W9-BHY-976

Grades 1-3

Games Galore

Math

Why practice key curriculum skills using games? Games provide the perfect opportunity for students to engage in active learning, take part in social interactions, and—let's not forget—have fun!

With math standards in mind, we designed each game in *Games Galore—Math* to add purpose to students' play. Through hands-on, partner, small-group, and whole-class games, your students will review key math concepts as well as foster communication, cooperation, problem-solving, and critical-thinking skills.

*Games Galore—Math* is also designed to save you time. The comprehensive table of contents conveniently lists each game by skill, so you can quickly find a perfect fit for your curriculum needs. Plus "How to Use This Book" (page 4) will familiarize you with the book's helpful design and easy-to-use contents. Enjoy, and let the games begin!

©2002 by THE EDUCATION CENTER, INC.
All rights reserved.
ISBN #1-56234-491-9

Manufactured in the United States

10 9 8 7 6 5 4 3 2 1

# Table of Contents

## Number & Operations

## Measurement

# How to Use This Book

What makes *Games Galore—Math* as exciting for you as it is for your students? The easy-to-use organization, of course! Each game is designed with the following features:

- **Skill:** Identify the skill in a snap.
- **Number of players:** Quickly note partner, small-group, and whole-class games.
- **Materials:** Round up needed supplies based on this handy reference.
- **Object of the game:** Decide if a game provides the skill practice your students need.
- **Playing the game:** Cleverly written to the student, these directions are printed on a white background so you can easily copy them and place them with the game for student reference.
- **Reproducible page:** Find a reproducible—such as a student record sheet, gameboard, or pattern—located on the page following each game description.

Some of the games will contain the following to make preparation or play even easier!

- **Teacher preparation:** If there is advanced preparation needed to set up the game, refer to these step-by-step instructions.
- **Variation:** Extend the life of a game by adjusting the rules, setup, skill, or difficulty.
- **Answer keys:** While many games rely on student knowledge and teacher monitoring, you will find necessary answer keys at the back of the book for handy reference.

# Right on Target!

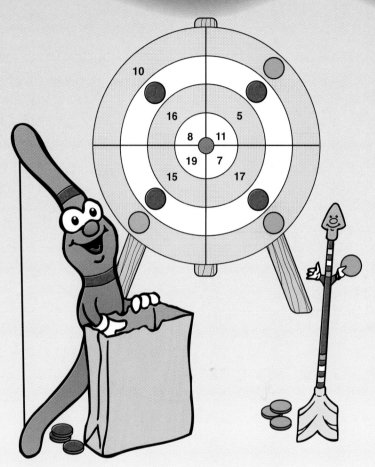

**Skill:** matching sets and numerals to 20

**Number of players:** 2

**Materials for each pair:**
- copy of page 6
- small paper sack filled with 25 small manipulatives (such as dried beans or buttons)
- 2 different sets of 12 game markers (such as 12 pennies and 12 dimes)

**Object of the game:**
to cover four spaces within the same ring or in a row cutting across rings by matching sets and numerals

**Playing the game:**
1. In turn, each player reaches into the bag and grabs a handful of items without looking.
2. The player counts the items, finds the matching number on the gameboard, and places one of his game markers on the matching number. If the number is not on the board or if the number has already been covered, the player's turn is over.
3. The items are returned to the bag before the next player takes a turn.
4. The first player to place a marker on four spaces within the same ring or in a row cutting across rings wins. If no player covers four connecting spaces, then the game is a draw.

©The Education Center, Inc.

**Variation:**

For addition practice, have students repeat Steps 1–3 until the gameboard is filled. Then each player adds the numbers covered by his markers. The player with the higher (or lower) total wins.

# Right on Target!

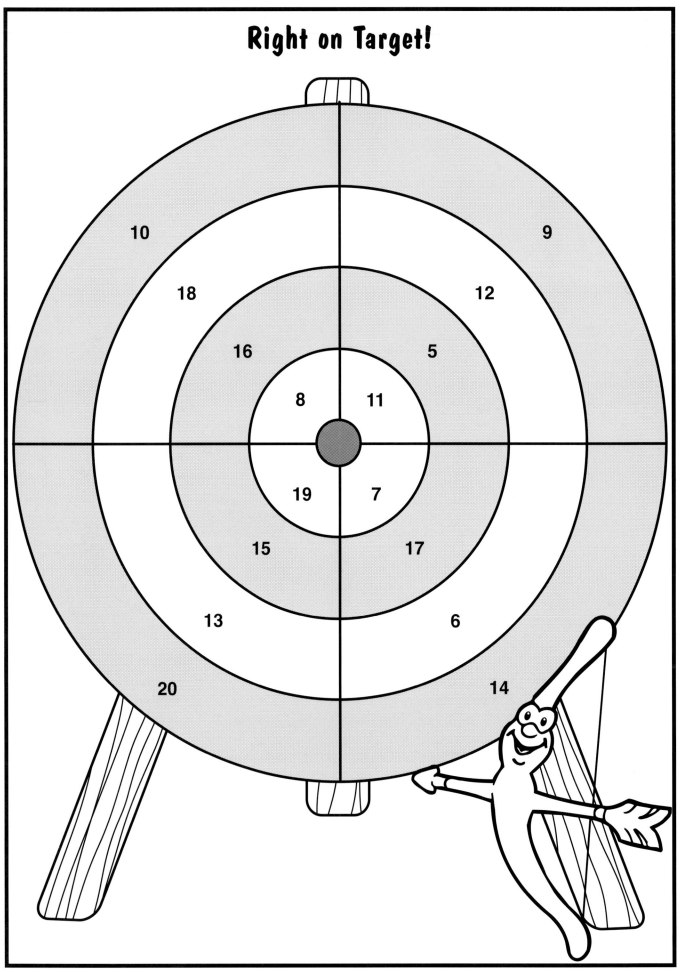

# Creepy-Crawlies

**Skill:** identifying ordinal words and positions

**Number of players:** 2

**Materials for each pair:**
- copy of page 8
- small paper clip
- sharpened pencil
- crayons

**Object of the game:**

to color all ten caterpillar segments based on ordinal position

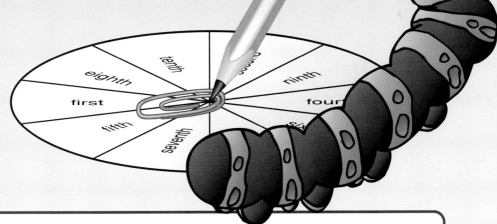

## Playing the game:

1. Player 1 uses the pencil and paper clip to spin the spinner.
2. Player 1 reads the ordinal number word, counts the sections of her caterpillar (including the head) to find the matching ordinal position, and colors the matching section.
3. Player 2 takes a turn in the same manner.
4. Players continue play. If the spinner stops between two words, the player may choose either word. If the spinner stops on a word and the matching section has been colored, the player's turn is over.
5. The first player to color all ten of her caterpillar sections wins the round.

©The Education Center, Inc.

Player 1 _____      Player 2 _____

# Creepy-Crawlies

### Round 1

### Round 2

### Round 3

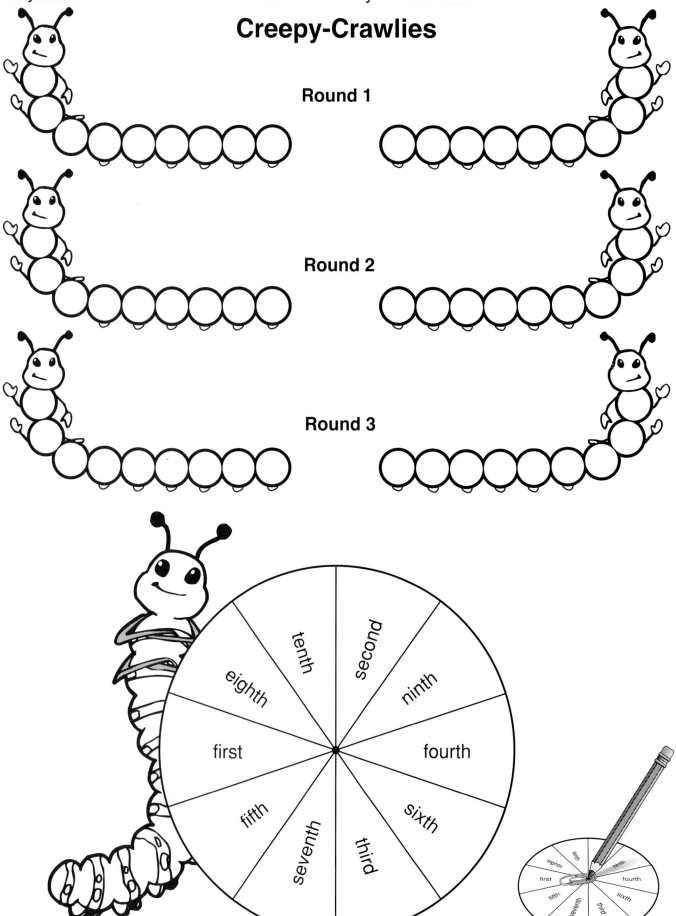

# Build-a-Bot

**Skill:** reading and spelling number words to 20

## s __ v __ n

Hmmm...

**Number of players:** 2

**Materials for each pair:**
- construction paper copy of the game cards, gameboard, and robot patterns on page 10 (cut out)
- sheet of paper
- pencil

**Object of the game:**

to guess and spell a number word before the robot is assembled

## Playing the game:
1. Stack the game cards facedown on the playing surface.
2. Player 1 draws a card, silently reads the number word, and draws a blank for each letter of the word on the paper.
3. Player 2 guesses a letter. If his guess is correct, Player 1 writes the letter in the appropriate blank. If his guess is incorrect, Player 1 records the letter and places a robot piece on the gameboard.
4. If Player 2 correctly guesses the word before the robot is built, he wins the round. If he does not guess the word before the robot is built, Player 1 wins the round. The number word is revealed and returned to the bottom of the stack.
5. Players alternate roles and repeat the game in the same manner until the end of game time, using a new word each time.

## Variation:
For practice with hyphenated number words, prepare number cards for 21–39 and give a copy to each pair.

## Game Cards

| one | two | three | four | five |
|-----|-----|-------|------|------|
| six | seven | eight | nine | ten |
| eleven | twelve | thirteen | fourteen | fifteen |
| sixteen | seventeen | eighteen | nineteen | twenty |

## Gameboard

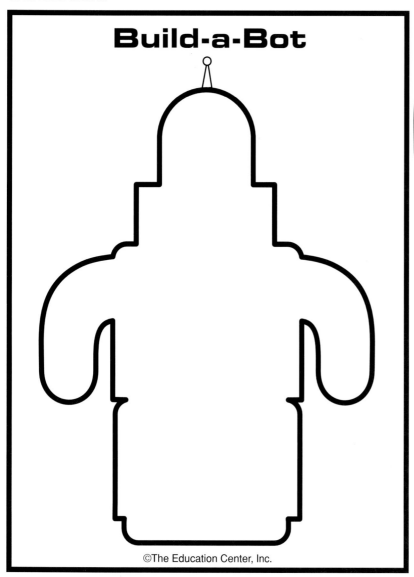

# Build-a-Bot

©The Education Center, Inc.

## Robot Patterns

# Race for the Place

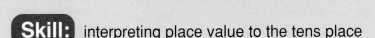

**Skill:** interpreting place value to the tens place

**Number of players:** 2

**Materials for each pair:**
- laminated copy of the gameboard on page 12
- overhead projection marker
- small paper clip
- pencil

**Object of the game:**

to mark five squares in a row (horizontally, vertically, or diagonally) by identifying place value

**Playing the game:**

1. Player 1 calls out a place value (ones or tens place) and then uses a pencil and paper clip to spin the spinner.
2. If the spinner stops on a number, the player marks an X in a numbered box that matches the resulting digit and place value called. If the spinner stops on "Lose a turn," the player's turn is over. If the spinner stops on "Choose a box," the player marks a box of his choice.
3. Player 2 takes a turn in the same manner, using O to mark his boxes.
4. Play continues until a player marks a row of five boxes in any direction or until time is up. If time is called before a player marks five boxes in a row, the player with more marked boxes is the winner.

**Variation:**

Have each player spin twice and combine the digits to form a two-digit number. For example, spinning the digits 3 and 4 could result in 34 or 43. Then direct the player to mark the corresponding numbered box on the gameboard.

# Race for the Place

| 0 | 1 | 2 | 3 | 4 | 5 | 6 | 7 | 8 | 9 |
|---|---|---|---|---|---|---|---|---|---|
| 10 | 11 | 12 | 13 | 14 | 15 | 16 | 17 | 18 | 19 |
| 20 | 21 | 22 | 23 | 24 | 25 | 26 | 27 | 28 | 29 |
| 30 | 31 | 32 | 33 | 34 | 35 | 36 | 37 | 38 | 39 |
| 40 | 41 | 42 | 43 | 44 | 45 | 46 | 47 | 48 | 49 |
| 50 | 51 | 52 | 53 | 54 | 55 | 56 | 57 | 58 | 59 |
| 60 | 61 | 62 | 63 | 64 | 65 | 66 | 67 | 68 | 69 |
| 70 | 71 | 72 | 73 | 74 | 75 | 76 | 77 | 78 | 79 |
| 80 | 81 | 82 | 83 | 84 | 85 | 86 | 87 | 88 | 89 |
| 90 | 91 | 92 | 93 | 94 | 95 | 96 | 97 | 98 | 99 |

# Place-Value Picnic

**Skill:** interpreting place value to the hundreds place

**Number of players:** whole class

**Materials:**
- copy of page 14 for each player
- scissors for each player
- glue for each player
- 15 game markers for each player
- 29 prepared index cards
- crayons for each player

**Teacher preparation:**

1. Program the index cards to show all the place-value possibilities: 0 ones to 9 ones, 0 tens to 9 tens, and 1 hundred to 9 hundreds. Shuffle the cards.
2. Distribute the remaining materials and have each student prepare a gameboard according to the directions on page 14.

**Object of the game:**

to cover three spaces in a row horizontally, vertically, or diagonally by identifying place value

**Playing the game:**

1. The caller draws a card and announces its value.
2. Each player finds each number on her gameboard with the corresponding value and covers it with a game marker. (For example, if "4 tens" is announced, each player covers all numbers on her gameboard with 4 in the tens place.)
3. The first player to cover three spaces in any direction announces "Place-value picnic" and becomes the caller for the next round of play.

©The Education Center, Inc.

**Variation:**

Have students exchange gameboards or change the object of the game to covering four corners or five spaces in a row.

Player_____

# Place-Value Picnic

Make a gameboard.
Color and cut out the number cards.
Mix up the cards; then glue each one
   on the gameboard.

©The Education Center, Inc. • *Games Galore* • *Math* • TEC2513

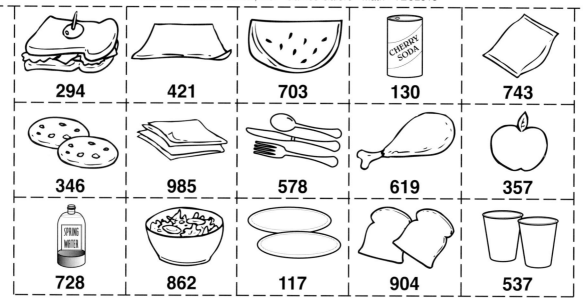

| | | |
|---|---|---|
| 294 | 421 | 703 | 130 | 743 |
| 346 | 985 | 578 | 619 | 357 |
| 728 | 862 | 117 | 904 | 537 |

14

# Poppin' Place Value

**Skills:** interpreting place value to the thousands place, comparing numbers

**Number of players:** 2

**Materials:**
- construction paper copy of the gameboard, numeral cards, and game markers on page 16 for each player (cut out)
- coin for each pair

**Object of the game:**

to cover the word *popcorn* by creating the larger or smaller number in each round

## Playing the game:
1. Each player places his game markers and numeral cards (shuffled and stacked facedown) beside his gameboard.
2. One player flips the coin to determine whether the higher number (heads) or lower number (tails) wins the round.
3. In turn, each player pulls a card from his stack and places it on his gameboard in the thousands, hundreds, tens, or ones place, trying to create the highest (or lowest) number possible.
4. Play continues until each player has formed a four-digit number.
5. Players compare numbers. The player with the higher (or lower) number places a game marker on his gameboard to cover a letter in the word *popcorn.*
6. New rounds are played in the same manner until one player wins the game by completely covering the word *popcorn.*

©The Education Center, Inc.

## Variation:

For place-value practice to the hundreds (or tens) place, white-out the word *thousands* (or *thousands* and *hundreds*) on the gameboard before duplicating page 16 for students. Then instruct students to form three- (or two-) digit numbers when playing the game.

**Gameboard**

# Poppin' Place Value

| Thousands | Hundreds | Tens | Ones |
|-----------|----------|------|------|

©The Education Center, Inc.

**Numeral Cards**

| 0 | 1 | 2 | 3 | 4 |
|---|---|---|---|---|
| 5 | 6 | 7 | 8 | 9 |

**Game Markers**

# Mail Matchup

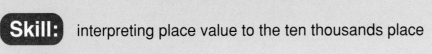

**Skill:** interpreting place value to the ten thousands place

**Number of players:** 2

**Materials for each pair:**
- copy of page 18
- pencil
- scissors

**Object of the game:**

to win more rounds by interpreting place value

## Playing the game:
1. Each player cuts out the envelopes and places them facedown in front of his gameboard.
2. For the first round of play, each player writes a different five-digit number for each house on the matching line.
3. In turn, each player chooses an envelope, reads the value aloud, and then checks to see if any of his house numbers match the value. If there is a match, the envelope is placed on the house. If there is not a match, the envelope is discarded. Only one envelope can be matched to each house.
4. Play continues in this manner until one player matches an envelope to each house or until all of the envelopes have been chosen.
5. At the end of play, the player with the most matches is the winner of the round. The winner records a point where indicated on the gameboard.
6. Two more rounds are played in the same manner, except players write different numbers for the homes each time. The player with more points after all three rounds wins the game.

©The Education Center, Inc.

Name _____

# Mail Matchup

Round 1 _____
Round 2 _____
Round 3 _____

Round 1 _____
Round 2 _____
Round 3 _____

Round 1 _____
Round 2 _____
Round 3 _____

Round 1 _____
Round 2 _____
Round 3 _____

**Points**

Round 1 _____
Round 2 _____
Round 3 _____

| 4 tens | 1 thousand | 7 ten thousands | 8 thousands | 8 tens | 9 thousands |
| 7 thousands | 3 ten thousands | 4 thousands | 4 ten thousands | 3 thousands | 1 ten thousand |
| 7 ones | 2 thousands | 5 hundreds | 6 thousands | 6 hundreds | 5 thousands |
| 0 tens | 2 hundreds | 3 hundreds | 5 ten thousands | 4 ones | 0 thousands |

# Winning Worms

**Skill:** comparing and ordering numbers to 50

**Number of players:** 2

**Materials for each pair:**
- construction paper copy of the gameboard and numbered cards on page 20 (cut out)
- small paper bag

**Object of the game:**

to fill a worm with the correct numbered cards

**Playing the game:**

1. Player 1 pulls a numbered game piece from the paper bag.
2. The game piece is placed in the corresponding space on the player's worm. If the corresponding space is already covered and the game piece cannot be played, it is returned to the bag and the player's turn is over.
3. Player 2 takes a turn in the same manner.
4. The first player to fill her worm wins the game.

©The Education Center, Inc.

**Variation:**

For more challenging practice, white-out the number ranges on the gameboard before duplicating page 20 for students. Then challenge the students in each pair to draw five numbered cards in turn and to be the first to arrange them on their worms in order from greatest to least (or least to greatest).

**Gameboard**

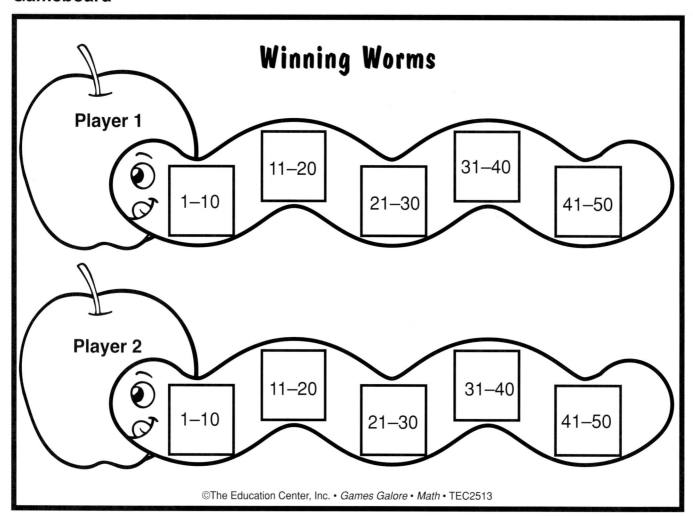

# Winning Worms

**Player 1**

1–10   11–20   21–30   31–40   41–50

**Player 2**

1–10   11–20   21–30   31–40   41–50

©The Education Center, Inc. • *Games Galore* • *Math* • TEC2513

**Game Pieces**

| 1 | 2 | 3 | 4 | 5 | 6 | 7 | 8 | 9 | 10 |
|---|---|---|---|---|---|---|---|---|---|
| 11 | 12 | 13 | 14 | 15 | 16 | 17 | 18 | 19 | 20 |
| 21 | 22 | 23 | 24 | 25 | 26 | 27 | 28 | 29 | 30 |
| 31 | 32 | 33 | 34 | 35 | 36 | 37 | 38 | 39 | 40 |
| 41 | 42 | 43 | 44 | 45 | 46 | 47 | 48 | 49 | 50 |

# Name That Number!

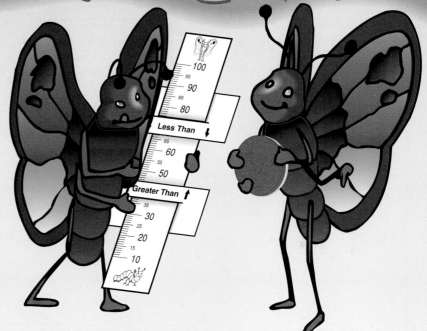

**Skill:** comparing two-digit numbers

**Number of players:** 2

**Materials for each pair:**
- copy of page 22
- scissors
- scrap paper
- pencil
- 50 tokens

**Teacher preparation:**

Direct student pairs to assemble the number line according to the directions on their copies of page 22.

**Object of the game:**

to guess a number in fewer tries

## Playing the game:

1. Player 1 writes a secret two-digit number on scrap paper.
2. Player 2 takes a token from the pile and then tries to guess the number.
3. Player 1 tells Player 2 whether his guess is greater than or less than the secret number.
4. Player 2 moves the appropriate slider on the number line to the guessed number. (For example, if Player 2 guesses the number 50 and Player 1 responds that the secret number is greater than 50, Player 2 moves the Greater Than slider to 50 on the number line.)
5. The round continues in this manner, with Player 2 taking a token before each guess.
6. When the correct number is guessed, Player 1 reveals the number and the players switch roles for another round.
7. The player with fewer tokens at the end of both rounds wins the game.

©The Education Center, Inc.

## Variation:

For practice with three-digit numbers, add a zero to each number on the number line before duplicating the page for students. Player 1 chooses a three-digit number that is a multiple of ten.

# How to assemble the number line:

1. Cut out the number line and the sliders along the bold lines.
2. Make a slit in each slider along the dotted line.
3. Slip the number line through each slider as shown.

## Sliders

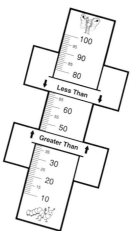

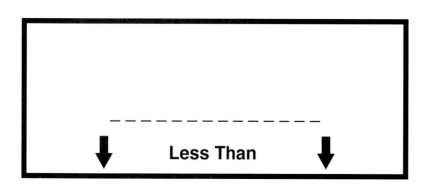

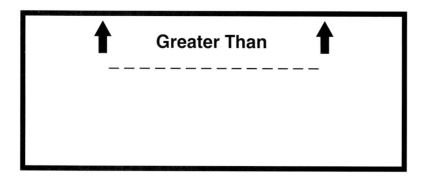

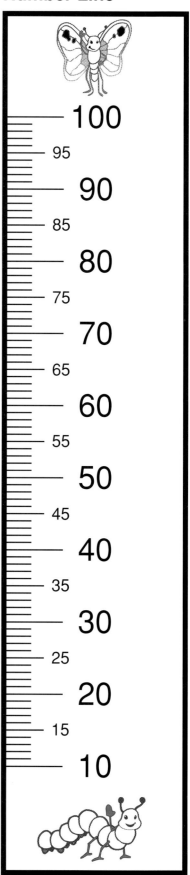

**Number Line**

# Yum-Yum! Bubble Gum!

**Skill:** identifying odd and even numbers

**Number of players:** 2–4

**Materials:**
- a copy of the gumball mat on page 24 for each player (colored and laminated if desired)
- 20 plastic chips for each player
- construction paper copy of the game pieces on page 20 (cut out) for each group
- small paper bag for each group

**Object of the game:**

to cover all gumballs in one machine by recognizing odd and even numbers

**Playing the game:**
1.  Put the numbered game pieces inside the bag.
2.  In turn, a player pulls a game piece from the bag, reads the number aloud, and covers a gumball in the corresponding gum machine with a plastic chip.
3.  The game piece is returned to the bag before the next player takes a turn.
4.  The first player to cover all the gumballs in one machine calls out "Yum-yum! Bubble gum!" and wins the game.

**Variation:**

For an added challenge, have players draw from a stack of math fact flash cards instead of using the game pieces. Have the player decide whether each card's answer is odd or even. The winner is the first player to cover all gumballs in both the odd and even machines.

Yum-Yum! Bubble Gum!

Odd

Even

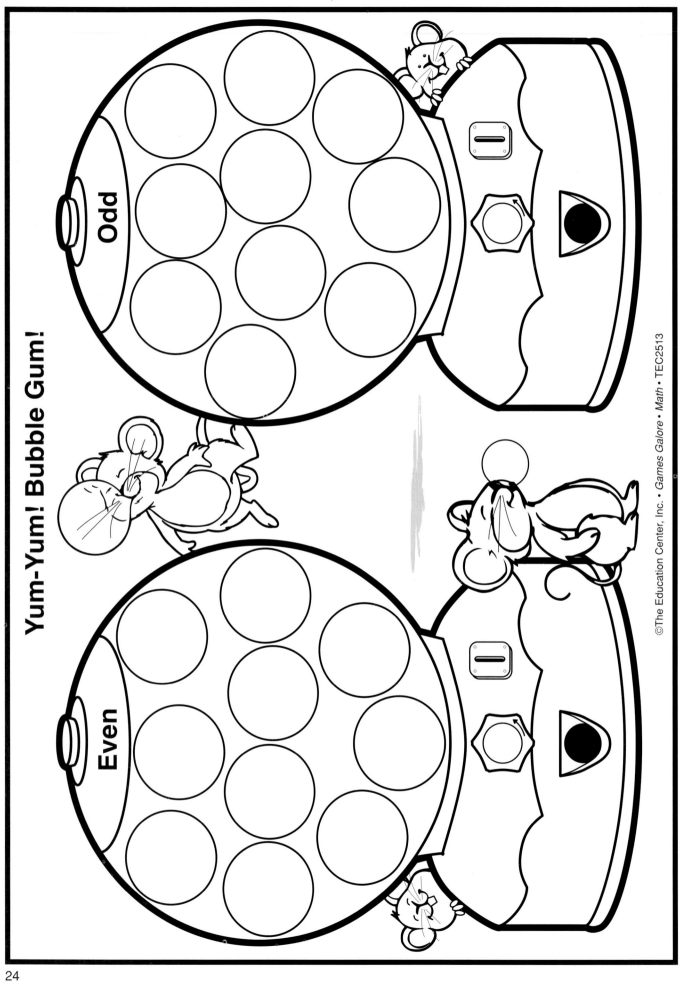

# Great Grapes

**Skill:** identifying odd and even numbers

**Number of players:** 2

**Materials for each pair:**
- copy of page 26
- green and purple crayons
- coin

**Object of the game:**

to color all the grapes in a bunch by identifying odd and even numbers

**Playing the game:**
1. Each player chooses a crayon.
2. In turn, each player flips the coin. If the coin lands on heads, the player colors a grape with an even number. If the coin lands on tails, she colors a grape with an odd number. (See the coin code.)
3. If a grape cannot be colored, the player's turn is over.
4. The first player to color all of her grapes wins.

©The Education Center, Inc.

**Variation:**

To simplify the game, place a self-adhesive dot on each side of the coin. Label one dot "odd" and the other dot "even." Then white-out numerals on the gameboard so that each grape will contain a one- or two-digit number.

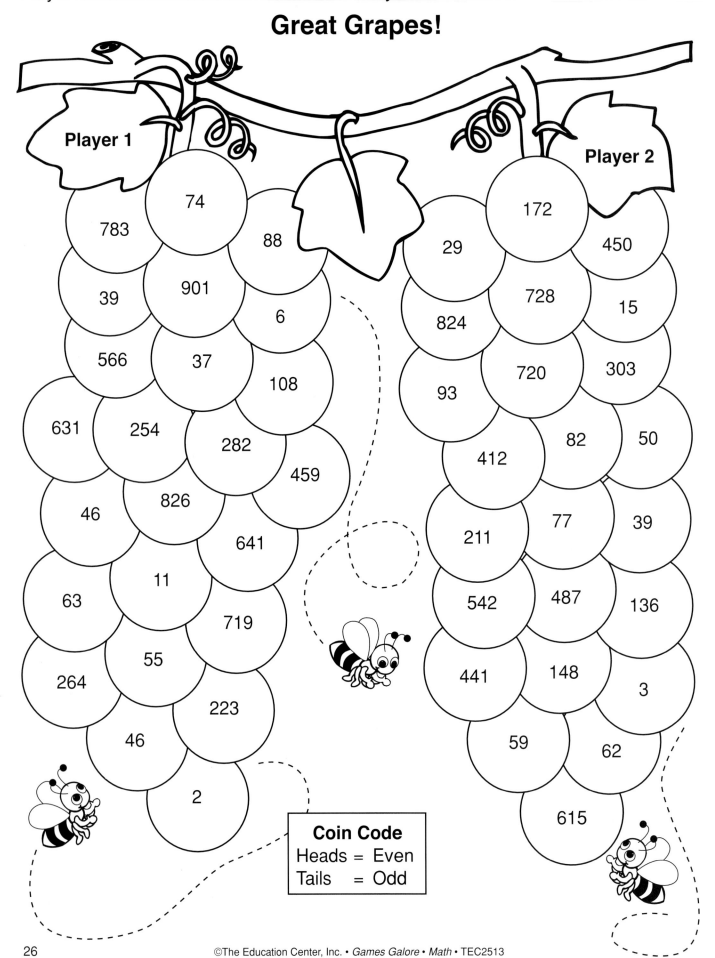

Player 1 _____ Player 2 _____

# Great Grapes!

**Player 1**

74
783
88
39
901
6
566
37
108
631
254
282
459
46
826
641
11
63
719
55
264
223
46
2

**Player 2**

172
29
450
728
15
824
720
303
93
82
50
412
77
39
211
542
487
136
441
148
3
59
62
615

| Coin Code |
| Heads = Even |
| Tails = Odd |

©The Education Center, Inc. • *Games Galore* • Math • TEC2513

# Square Up

**Skill:** reviewing addition facts

**Number of players:** 2

**Materials:**
- copy of page 28
- deck of playing cards with face cards removed
- 2 sets of 16 square tiles (a different color for each player)

**Object of the game:**

to be the first player to place four tiles on the gameboard in the form of a square

**Playing the game:**
1. Shuffle the cards and stack them facedown on the playing surface.
2. Player 1 draws two cards and adds the numbers shown. Player 2 checks his answer by counting the symbols on the cards. If the answer is correct, Player 1 places a tile on the gameboard. If the answer is incorrect, his turn is over.
3. Player 2 takes a turn in the same manner.
4. Players may reshuffle the cards and restack them as needed.
5. Play continues until one player wins the game by placing four tiles on the gameboard in the form of a square. If neither player is able to form a square, the game is a draw.

**Variation:**

For multiplication practice, instruct players to multiply the numbers shown on the cards and have opponents use a calculator or multiplication chart to check answers.

# Square Up

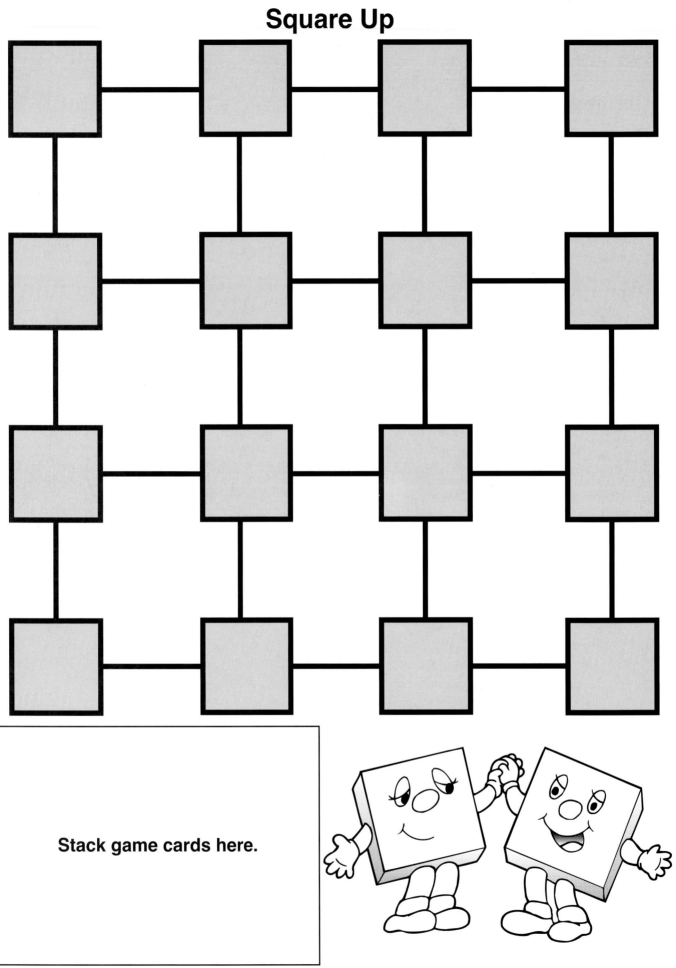

Stack game cards here.

# Rain Forest Race

**Skills:** computing basic math problems, comparing numbers

**Number of players:** 2

**Materials for each pair:**
- copy of page 30
- 2 game markers
- set of flash cards featuring the desired type of computation

**Object of the game:**
to reach the top of the rain forest by comparing answers to basic math facts

$7 + 2 = 9$

$1 + 2 = 3$

## Playing the game:
1. Each player places his marker on Start.
2. Each player pulls a flash card from the bottom of the stack and solves the problem.
3. The players compare answers. The player with the higher answer moves up two spaces. The player with the lower answer moves up one space. If the answers are equal, each player remains in his space.
4. Play continues in this manner.
5. The first player to reach the top of the canopy wins the game.

# Rain Forest Race

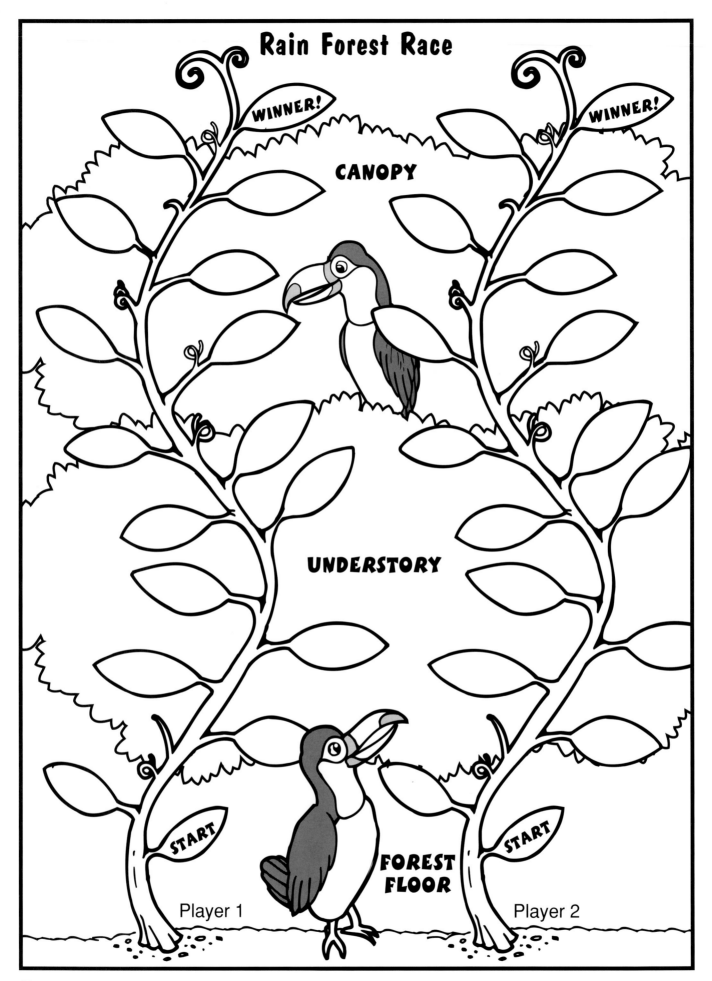

# Round Up!

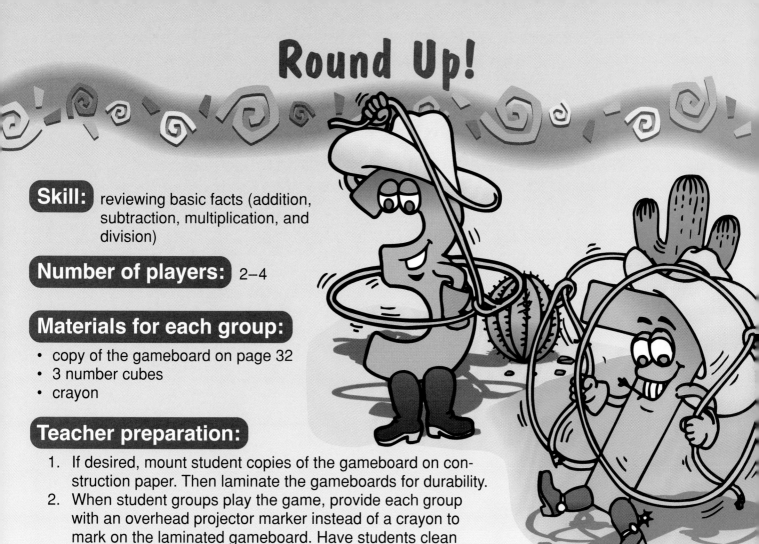

**Skill:** reviewing basic facts (addition, subtraction, multiplication, and division)

**Number of players:** 2–4

**Materials for each group:**
- copy of the gameboard on page 32
- 3 number cubes
- crayon

**Teacher preparation:**

1. If desired, mount student copies of the gameboard on construction paper. Then laminate the gameboards for durability.
2. When student groups play the game, provide each group with an overhead projector marker instead of a crayon to mark on the laminated gameboard. Have students clean their gameboards at the end of game time.

**Object of the game:**

to round up the most points by computing number combinations

## Playing the game:

1. Each player rolls the number cubes. The student with the highest roll becomes Player 1, the student with the next-highest roll becomes Player 2, and so on.
2. Player 1 rolls the number cubes. Then he manipulates the numbers by using any operation or combination of operations to get a number that appears on the gameboard. For example, if 5, 4, and 2 are rolled, possible combinations would include $(5 + 4) - 2 = 7$ and $(5 \times 2) \times 4 = 40$.
3. If Player 1's answer is correct and appears on the gameboard, he circles the number.
4. Player 2 then repeats Steps 2 and 3.
5. A player earns one point for each circled number that is adjacent to the number he marks.
6. If a player is unable to circle a number, his turn is over.
7. Play continues until each number on the gameboard has been circled or until the end of game time. The player who rounds up the most points wins.

# Round Up!

| 1 | 2 | 3 | 4 | 5 | 6 | 7 | 8 | 9 | 10 |
|---|---|---|---|---|---|---|---|---|-----|
| 11 | 12 | 13 | 14 | 15 | 16 | 17 | 18 | 19 | 20 |
| 21 | 22 | 23 | 24 | 25 | 26 | 27 | 28 | 29 | 30 |
| 31 | 32 | 33 | 34 | 35 | 36 | 37 | 38 | 39 | 40 |
| 41 | 42 | 44 | 45 | 48 | 50 | 54 | 55 | 60 | 64 |
| 66 | 72 | 75 | 80 | 90 | 96 | 100 | 108 | 120 | 125 |

# Battle of the Bugs

**Skill:** adding (or subtracting) two-digit numbers with regrouping

**Number of players:** 2

**Materials for each player:**
- construction paper copy of the game cards on page 34 (cut out)
- lined paper
- pencil
- access to a calculator

**Teacher preparation:**

Determine for students whether they are to add or subtract while playing the game.

**Object of the game:**

to earn more points by adding (or subtracting) correctly

**Playing the game:**
1. Each player shuffles her cards and stacks them facedown.
2. Each player draws two cards and adds (or subtracts) the numbers shown.
3. Opponents check each other's answers with a calculator.
4. If a player's answer is correct, she gets one point. If she had to regroup to solve the problem, she gets another point. If a player's answer is incorrect, she doesn't get any points.
5. The cards are placed in a discard pile.
6. Play continues until all of the cards have been used. The player with more points wins.

**Variation:**

Have students play the game as directed but allow them to earn an additional point for having the largest sum (or difference).

**Game Cards**

©The Education Center, Inc. • *Games Galore* • *Math* • TEC2513

# "Tree-mendous" Subtraction

**Skill:** subtracting numbers with regrouping

**Number of players:** 2

**Materials for each pair:**
- copy of page 36 (numbers cut out)
- 2 pencils
- calculator (optional)

**Object of the game:**

to get the lower score by subtracting numbers

## Playing the game:

1. Place the number cards facedown on the playing surface.
2. For the first round of play, Player 1 draws a number card, creates a math problem by copying the number shown into the provided boxes, and solves the problem.
3. Player 2 checks his opponent's answer. Any necessary changes are made, and the card is placed in a discard pile.
4. Player 2 draws a card and takes a turn in the same manner.
5. Play continues for the next nine rounds. For each round, a student uses his answer from the previous round of play as the larger number of his next subtraction problem.
6. The student with the lower score after ten rounds of play wins the game.

©The Education Center, Inc.

## Variation:

For addition practice, make a copy of page 36. White-out "Tree-mendous Subtraction" and change each subtraction sign to an addition sign. Then duplicate the page for students. Students play the game in the same manner. The player with the higher score wins.

Player 1 _____     Player 2 _____

# "Tree-mendous" Subtraction

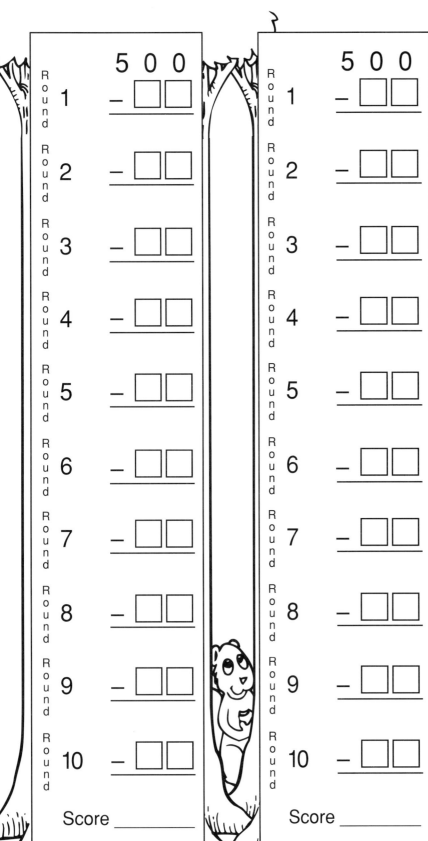

| Round | | 5 0 0 |
|---|---|---|
| 1 | − | ☐ ☐ |
| 2 | − | ☐ ☐ |
| 3 | − | ☐ ☐ |
| 4 | − | ☐ ☐ |
| 5 | − | ☐ ☐ |
| 6 | − | ☐ ☐ |
| 7 | − | ☐ ☐ |
| 8 | − | ☐ ☐ |
| 9 | − | ☐ ☐ |
| 10 | − | ☐ ☐ |

Score _____

| Round | | 5 0 0 |
|---|---|---|
| 1 | − | ☐ ☐ |
| 2 | − | ☐ ☐ |
| 3 | − | ☐ ☐ |
| 4 | − | ☐ ☐ |
| 5 | − | ☐ ☐ |
| 6 | − | ☐ ☐ |
| 7 | − | ☐ ☐ |
| 8 | − | ☐ ☐ |
| 9 | − | ☐ ☐ |
| 10 | − | ☐ ☐ |

Score _____

| | |
|---|---|
| 11 | 28 |
| 35 | 45 |
| 19 | 16 |
| 31 | 38 |
| 27 | 44 |
| 16 | 33 |
| 46 | 14 |
| 59 | 32 |
| 57 | 25 |
| 18 | 55 |

# Snail Trail

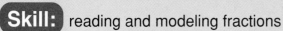

**Skill:** reading and modeling fractions

**Number of players:** 2

**Materials for each pair:**
- copy of page 38
- die
- 2 game markers
- four prepared 6" construction paper circles

**Teacher preparation:**
1. Cut out four six-inch circles from different-colored construction paper.
2. Leave one circle whole. Cut one circle into halves, one into thirds, and one into fourths.

**Object of the game:**
to be the first player to arrive at Snail's house by reading and modeling fractions along the trail

**Playing the game:**
1. The players place their markers on Start, and then they place the whole and cut circles beside the gameboard.
2. Player 1 rolls the die and moves ahead the number of spaces shown. Then he reads the fraction on the space and uses parts of the cut circles to model the fraction on top of the whole circle.
3. If both players agree the answer is correct, Player 1 remains in that spot. If the answer is incorrect, Player 1 moves back to his original spot.
4. Player 2 takes a turn in the same manner. (If a player lands on the same spot that his partner is on, he must move back one space.)
5. Alternate play continues until one player wins by reaching Snail's house.

# Snail Trail

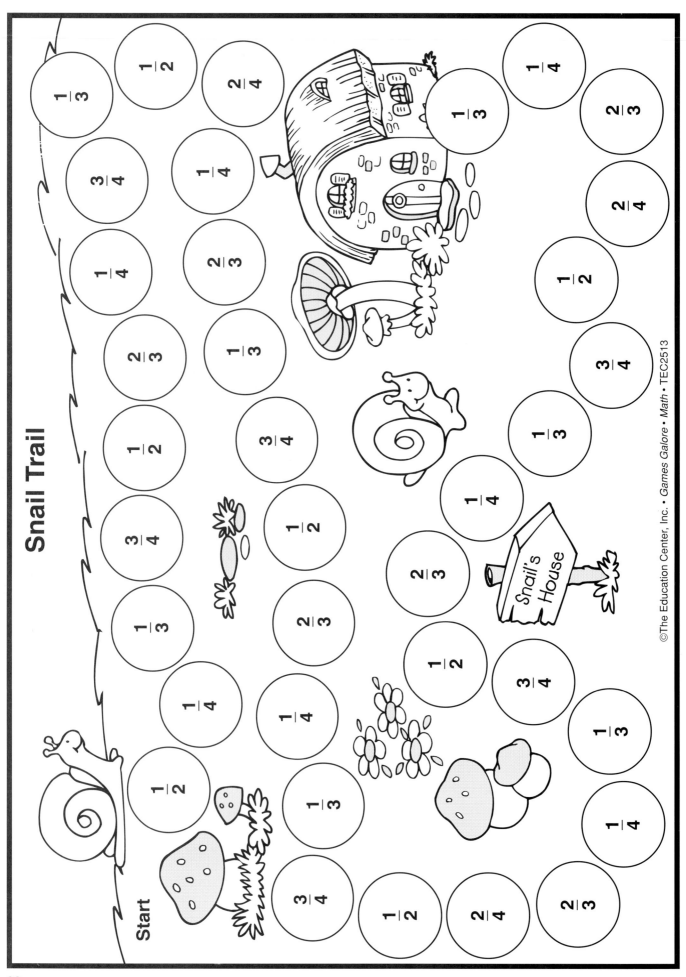

Start

Snail's House

# Fraction Traction

**Skill:** identifying fractional parts of wholes

**Number of players:** 2–4

**Materials:**
- copy of page 40 for each player
- crayon or colored pencil for each player
- pair of number cubes for each group

**Object of the game:**
to color eight whole tires by identifying the correct fractional parts

## Playing the game:

1. Player 1 rolls the number cubes and forms a fraction with the numbers shown using the lower number for the numerator and the higher number for the denominator.
2. Player 1 colors the parts on a single tire to represent the fraction. (If possible, he may color an equivalent fraction.)
3. If the player rolls a double, he may color a whole tire.
4. If a player has no room to color the amount shown, his turn is over.
5. Remaining players take turns in the same manner. Play rotates among the group until the game's end.
6. The first player to completely color eight tires wins.

## Variation:

For a more challenging game, allow each player to color multiple tires that represent the fraction he rolls. For example, if $^3/_5$ is rolled, the player may color $^2/_5$ of one tire and $^1/_5$ of another. Or allow students to color equivalent fractional parts.

# Fraction Traction

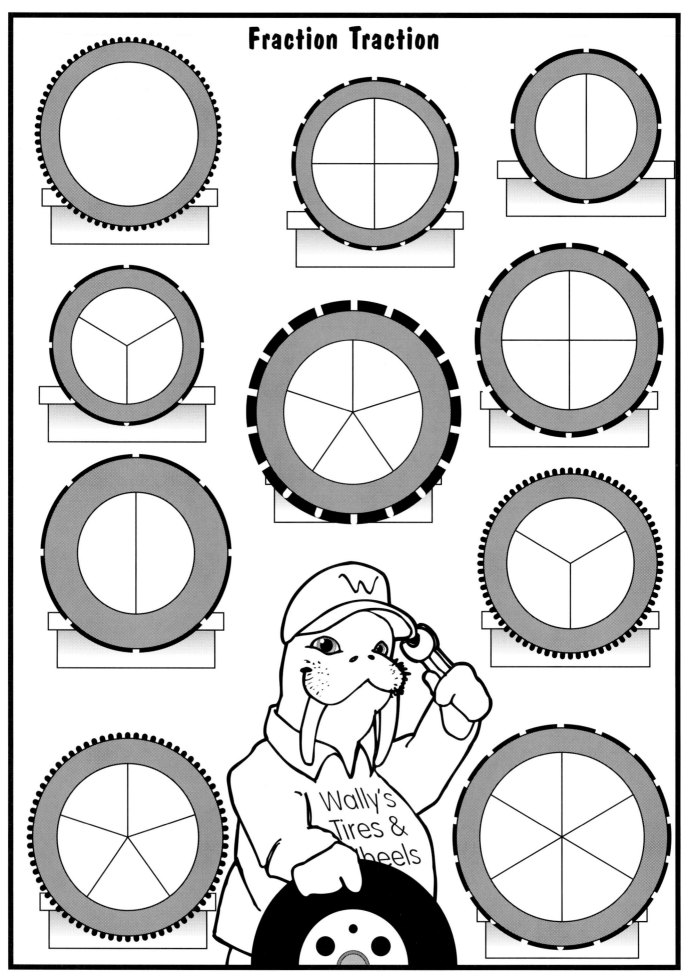

# Bit by Bit

**Skill:** measuring length to the nearest centimeter

**Number of players:** 2

**Materials for each pair:**
- copy of page 42
- die
- centimeter ruler
- 2 colored pencils

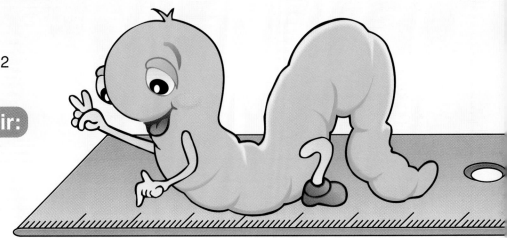

**Object of the game:**

to be the first player to reach the end of the gameboard by moving a specified number of centimeters at a time

**Playing the game:**
1. Player 1 rolls the die to determine the length of the line he can draw (see code). He starts at the • and draws his line.
2. Player 2 takes a turn in the same manner.
3. Each player must draw the entire line length. A line may not be broken or go outside the game trail. If a line cannot be drawn within the boundaries, the turn is lost.
4. The first player to reach the ★ wins.

**Variation:**

For practice with measuring in inches, white-out each reference to centimeters in the code on page 42 and replace it with "in." Then duplicate the page for students. Provide each student pair with an inch ruler and have the pair play the game in the same manner.

Player 1 _____    Player 2 _____

# Bit by Bit

**Code**

| | |
|---|---|
| 1 = 1 cm | 4 = 4 cm |
| 2 = 2 cm | 5 = 5 cm |
| 3 = 3 cm | 6 = 0 cm |

Start here.

# Catch of the Day

**Skill:** estimating and measuring to the nearest half inch

**Number of players:** 2

**Materials for each pair:**
- construction paper copy of the fish patterns on page 44
- scissors
- inch ruler

**Object of the game:**

to "catch" more fish by estimating and measuring your catch correctly

## Playing the game:
1. Cut out the fish and place them on the playing surface in random order.
2. Player 1 chooses any fish and estimates its length to the nearest half inch.
3. Player 2 measures between the circles on the fish to see how close Player 1's estimate is to the correct length.
4. If Player 1's estimate matches the fish's length, he gets to keep the fish. If the estimate doesn't match, the fish is placed in a discard pile.
5. Player 2 takes a turn in the same manner.
6. Alternate play continues until all of the fish have been measured. The player who "catches" more fish wins the game. If both players catch the same amount of fish, the game is a tie.

## Variation:

For more strategic play, change the object of the game to making the longer line of "caught" fish.

# Fish Patterns

# Perimeter Pairs

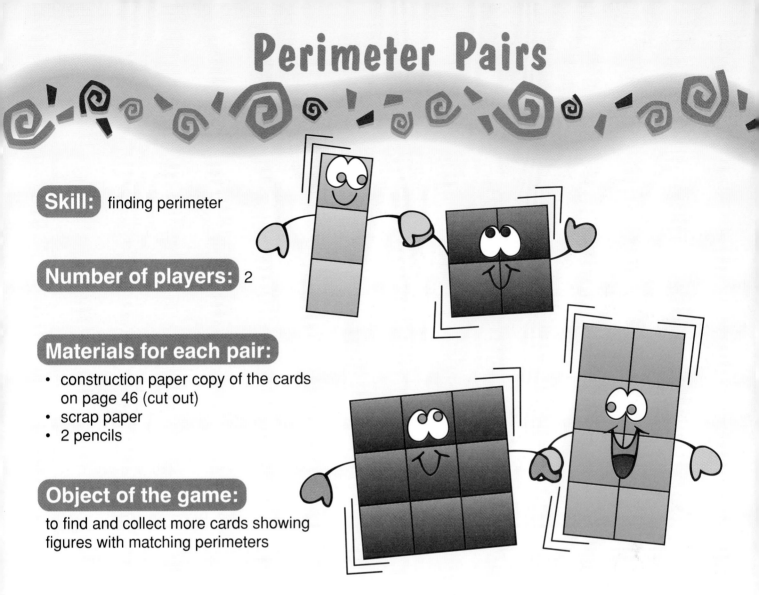

**Skill:** finding perimeter

**Number of players:** 2

**Materials for each pair:**
- construction paper copy of the cards on page 46 (cut out)
- scrap paper
- 2 pencils

**Object of the game:**

to find and collect more cards showing figures with matching perimeters

**Playing the game:**
1. Place the cards facedown in rows and columns on the playing surface.
2. In turn, each player flips two cards and finds the perimeter of each figure shown by adding the lengths of the sides. If the perimeters are equal, she keeps the cards. If not, she flips them over.
3. Alternate play continues in this manner. The player who collects more cards wins.

©The Education Center, Inc.

**Variation:**

For a more challenging game, white-out the lengths of the sides on each figure before duplicating the game cards for students.

# Game Cards

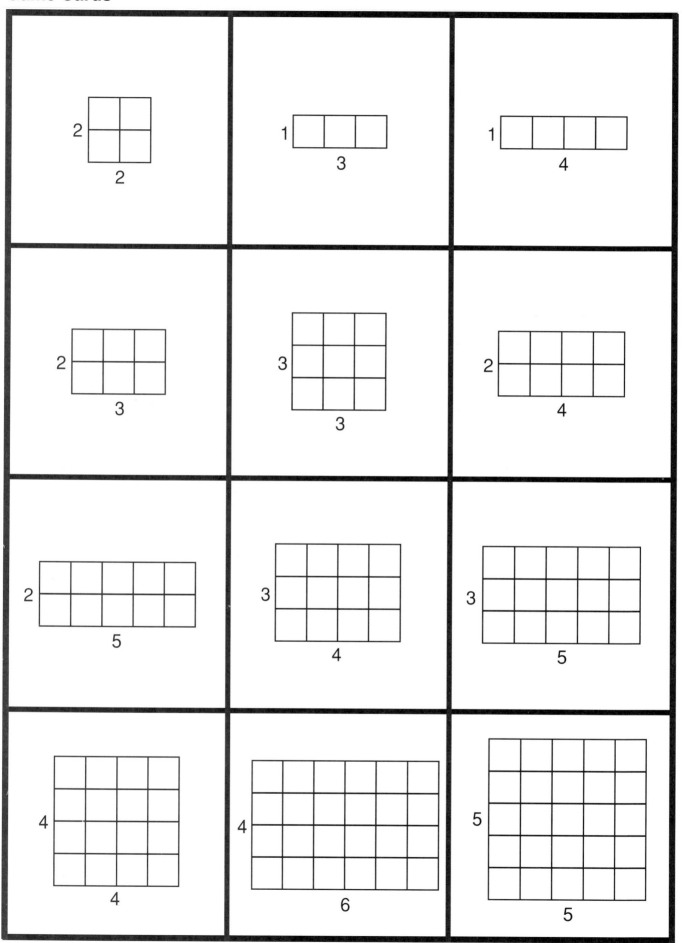

# Squares and Rectangles

**Skill:** finding area

**Number of players:** 2

**Materials:**
- construction paper copy of the cards on page 48 for each pair (cut out)
- centimeter graph paper for each player
- crayon for each player

**Object of the game:**

to color a larger area

**Playing the game:**

1. Stack the playing cards facedown on the playing surface.
2. Player 1 draws a card, colors a figure on her graph paper that matches the shape and area shown, and then places the card in a discard pile.
3. Player 2 takes a turn in the same manner.
4. Alternate play continues with each player adding on to her previous figure. If it is impossible for the player to create a figure, her turn is over.
5. The game ends when all cards have been drawn. The player with the larger area colored wins.

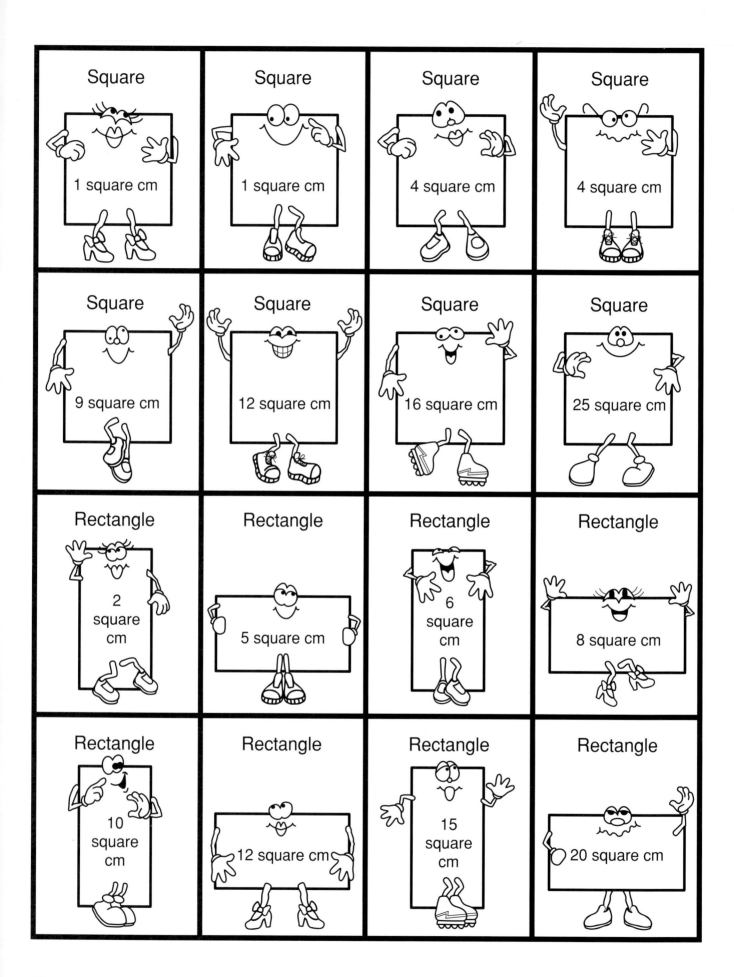

Square — 1 square cm

Square — 1 square cm

Square — 4 square cm

Square — 4 square cm

Square — 9 square cm

Square — 12 square cm

Square — 16 square cm

Square — 25 square cm

Rectangle — 2 square cm

Rectangle — 5 square cm

Rectangle — 6 square cm

Rectangle — 8 square cm

Rectangle — 10 square cm

Rectangle — 12 square cm

Rectangle — 15 square cm

Rectangle — 20 square cm

# "Mass-ive" Measurement

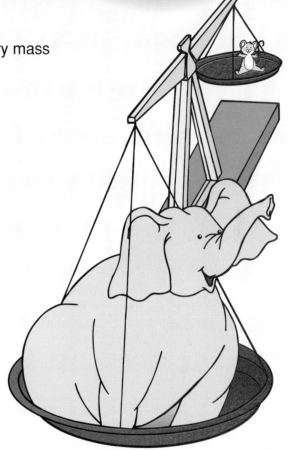

**Skill:** identifying reasonable units of customary mass

**Number of players:** 2

**Materials for each pair:**
- construction paper copy of the game cards on page 50 (cut out)
- balance scale
- 18 counters or manipulatives
- copy of the answer key on page 95

**Object of the game:**

to collect more manipulatives by correctly identifying the appropriate unit of mass

**Playing the game:**

1. Shuffle the cards and stack them facedown.
2. Player 1 chooses a card and states the most appropriate unit (ounces or pounds) for weighing the object shown. If Player 1 chooses the "Lose a turn" card, her turn is over.
3. Player 2 looks at the key to check Player 1's answer. If Player 1 is correct, she places a counter on her side of the balance. If she is not correct, her turn is over.
4. Player 2 takes a turn in the same manner.
5. Play continues until all the cards have been drawn. The player who has more counters on her side of the scale wins.

**Variation:**

For practice with metric units of mass, have players determine whether to weigh each object in grams or kilograms. Prepare an answer key for the new game. (A paper clip weighs about one gram. A textbook weighs about one kilogram.)

| | | | | |
|---|---|---|---|---|
| **1** bag of chips | **2** marker | **3** desk | **4** dog | **5** watermelon |
| **6** bag of apples | **7** child | **8** letter | **9** bicycle | **10** stick of butter |
| **11** mouse | **12** eyeglasses | **13** teddy bear | **14** tiger | **15** bag of potatoes |
| **16** candy bar | **17** bunch of bananas | **18** computer | **Lose a turn.** | **Lose a turn.** |

# High Rollers

**Skill:** comparing cups, pints, quarts, and gallons

**Number of players:** 2

**Materials for each player:**
- copy of page 52
- paper
- pencil
- scissors
- glue

**Teacher preparation:**

Post the following information for students to refer to while playing the game:
1 gallon = 4 quarts
1 quart = 2 pints
1 pint = 2 cups

**Object of the game:**

to earn ten points by rolling the greatest capacities

**Playing the game:**

1. Assemble the dice as directed on page 52.
2. Each player rolls his dice. Players read the number and the unit of capacity shown; then they compare capacity amounts.
3. The player with the higher capacity earns a point. If the amounts are equal, both players earn a point.
4. The game continues until one player wins by earning ten points.

**Directions:**

1. Carefully cut out the die patterns along the bold lines.
2. Fold the patterns along the thin lines to form cubes.
3. Glue each tab on the inside of each die.

cup(s)

cup(s)

pint(s)

quart(s)

gallon(s)

pint(s)

5

1

2

3

4

<u>6</u>

# The Fahrenheit Challenge

**Skill:** reading a thermometer

**Number of players:** 2

**Materials for each pair:**
- copy of page 54
- red crayon
- pencil
- small paper clip

**Object of the game:**

to be the first player to reach 100°F without going over.

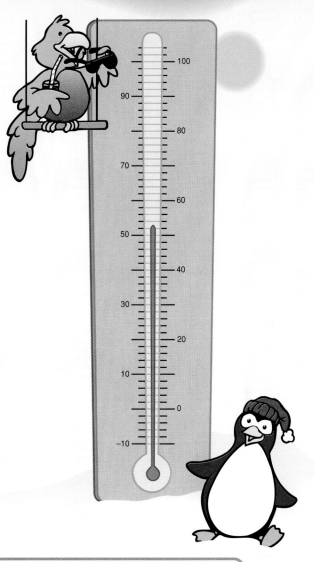

## Playing the game:
1. Player 1 uses the pencil and paper clip to spin the spinner.
2. Player 1 then colors the bulb at the bottom of his thermometer and the number of degrees above it as shown on the spinner.
3. Player 2 takes a turn in the same manner.
4. With each spin, players add to their existing thermometer readings.
5. Alternating play continues until one player reaches 100°F without going over.

©The Education Center, Inc.

## Variation:

For practice reading smaller degree increments, white-out the numbers 10–30 on the spinner and replace them with the numbers 1–4, 6, and 7 before duplicating the gameboard for students.

Player 1 _____    Player 2 _____

# The Fahrenheit Challenge

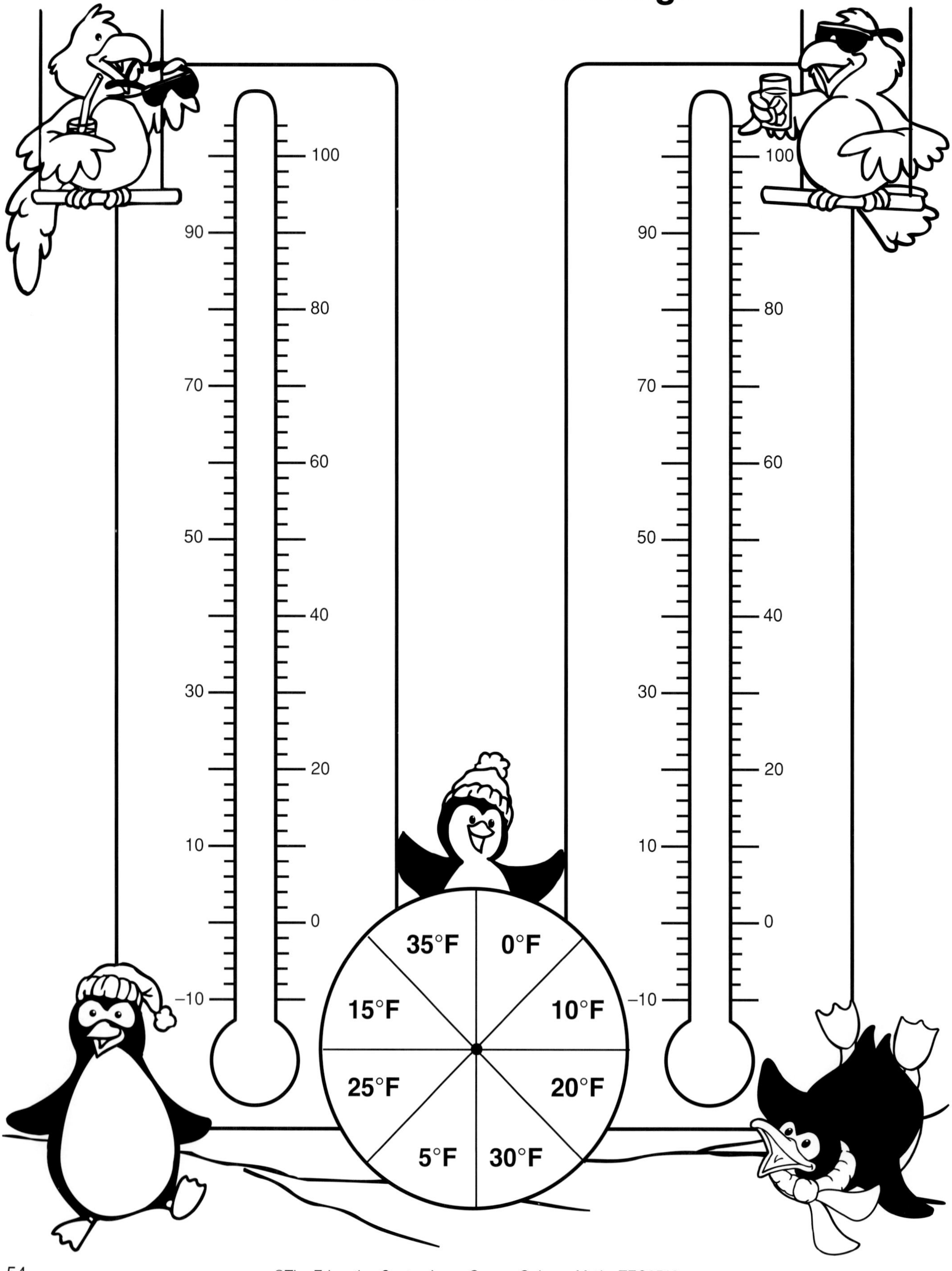

100
90
80
70
60
50
40
30
20
10
0
−10

100
90
80
70
60
50
40
30
20
10
0
−10

| 35°F | 0°F |
| 15°F | 10°F |
| 25°F | 20°F |
| 5°F | 30°F |

54

# Timeline

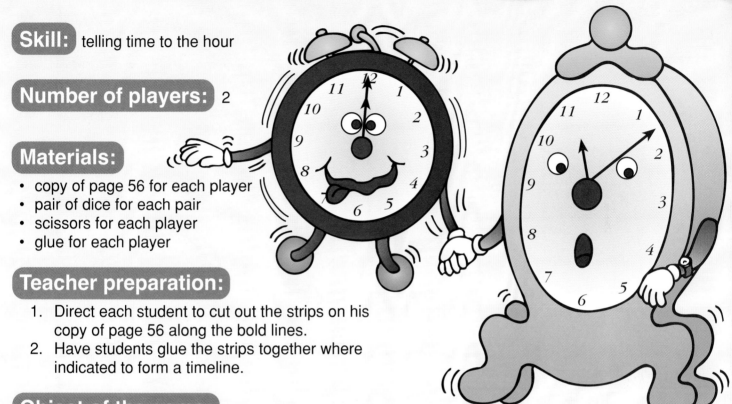

**Skill:** telling time to the hour

**Number of players:** 2

**Materials:**
- copy of page 56 for each player
- pair of dice for each pair
- scissors for each player
- glue for each player

**Teacher preparation:**
1. Direct each student to cut out the strips on his copy of page 56 along the bold lines.
2. Have students glue the strips together where indicated to form a timeline.

**Object of the game:**

to be the first player to model each time on the timeline

**Playing the game:**
1. In turn, each player rolls the dice, finds the clock on her timeline that corresponds with the number rolled, and draws hands to show the time.
2. If a player rolls a number that she has already rolled, her turn is over.
3. The first player to complete her timeline wins.

©The Education Center, Inc.

**Variation:**

For practice writing both analog and digital time, white-out the digital time above each clock before duplicating page 56 for students. Then have each player write the analog and digital time when the corresponding number is rolled.

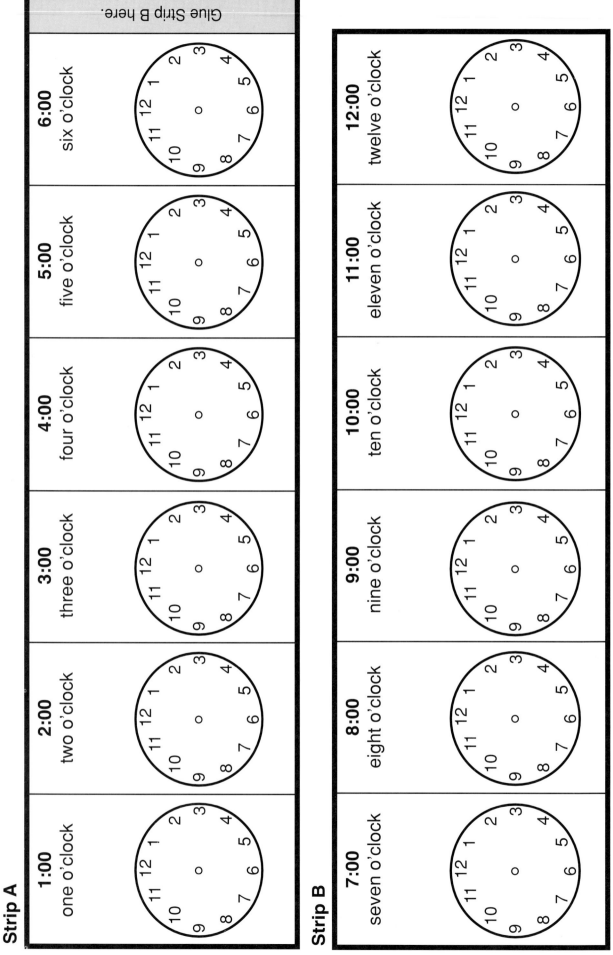

**Strip A**

Glue Strip B here.

| 1:00 | 2:00 | 3:00 | 4:00 | 5:00 | 6:00 |
| one o'clock | two o'clock | three o'clock | four o'clock | five o'clock | six o'clock |

**Strip B**

| 7:00 | 8:00 | 9:00 | 10:00 | 11:00 | 12:00 |
| seven o'clock | eight o'clock | nine o'clock | ten o'clock | eleven o'clock | twelve o'clock |

©The Education Center, Inc. • *Games Galore* • *Math* • TEC2513

# Wipe Out!

**Skill:** telling time

**Number of players:** 2–4

**Materials for each group:**
- prepared game cards

## Teacher preparation:

1. Make a copy of page 58. Program the clock on each game card with a desired time.
2. Fill in the answer key with the corresponding times.
3. Make two construction paper copies of the programmed page for each group of players.
4. Cut apart the game cards.

## Object of the game:

to collect the most cards by telling time correctly

## Playing the game:

1. Put the answer keys aside and stack the cards facedown in the center of the playing surface.
2. Player 1 pulls a card and states the time shown. The player to his right checks the answer key. If Player 1 is correct, he lays the card faceup in front of him. If he is not, he places the card at the bottom of the deck.
3. If Player 1 receives a "Surf's Up!" or a "Wipe Out!" card, he must follow the directions on the card.
4. The player to the left takes a turn in the same manner.
5. Play continues until all the cards have been pulled. The player who collects the most cards wins.

## Variation:

For a matching game, players arrange only the clockface cards facedown on a playing surface. In turn, each player flips two cards and states the time shown on each one. If the cards match, he keeps them. If they do not, he returns them to their original positions. The game is over when all the cards have been paired. The player with the most cards wins.

# Game Cards

**Surf's Up!**
Take the top card from each player's stack.

**Wipe Out!**
Keep this card. Return your other cards to the bottom of the deck.

**Answer Key**

1.
2.
3.
4.
5.
6.
7.
8.
9.
10.
11.
12.
13.
14.
15.
16.

# It's About Time

**Skills:** telling time to five minutes, elapsed time

**Number of players:** 2–4

**Materials:**
- white construction paper copy of page 60 for each player
- metal brad for each player
- scissors for each player
- crayons for each player
- game marker for each player
- access to a hole puncher
- die for each group

**Object of the game:**

to be the first player to reach 6:00 by modeling the correct times

**Playing the game:**

1. Assemble your clock as directed on page 60.
2. Each player sets his clock to 12:00 and places his game marker on the space directly above the 12.
3. Player 1 rolls the die and moves his token that number of spaces in a clockwise direction around the clock trail.
4. Player 1 reads the square he lands on and moves the hands of his clock forward and backward to the corresponding time.
5. Other players check Player 1's clock for accuracy. After players agree, Player 2 takes a turn in the same manner.
6. Play rotates among the players. The first player to reach 6:00 wins the game.

**Variation:**

For practice telling time to the minute, white-out and change the numbers of minutes on the game clock to numbers that are not multiples of five.

## Directions:

1. Color and cut out the clock face and clock hands.
2. Punch a hole in each clock hand where indicated.
3. Thread the minute hand and then the hour hand onto the brad.
4. Poke the brad into the center of the clock face (the white box) and fasten.

**Clock Face**

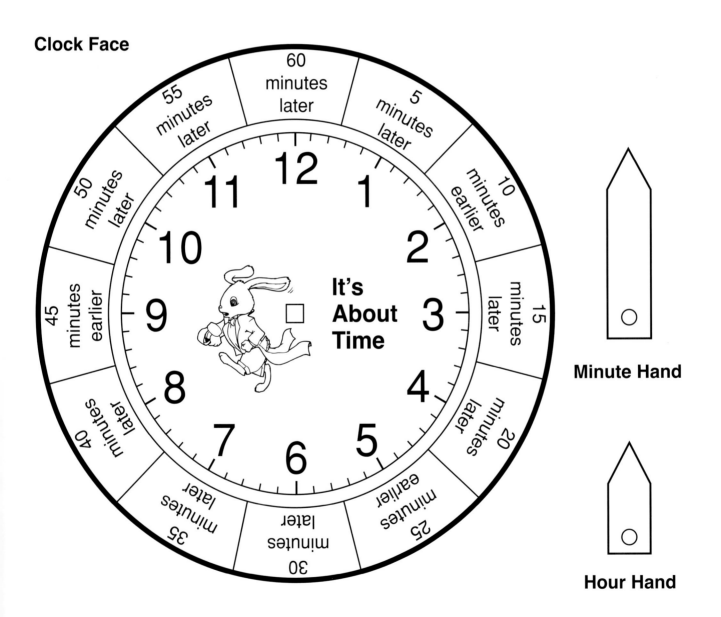

**Minute Hand**

**Hour Hand**

# Coin Collectors

**Skills:** counting coin values, comparing money amounts

**Number of players:** 2

**Materials for each pair:**
- 2 prepared construction paper copies of the coin cards on page 62
- resealable plastic bag
- die

**Teacher preparation:**
1. Cut out and laminate the coin cards for each pair.
2. Store each pair's cards in the resealable plastic bag.

**Object of the game:**
to collect more coin cards by counting coin values and comparing money amounts

**Playing the game:**
1. Place each coin card facedown on a playing surface.
2. In turn, a player rolls the die.
3. Each player takes the corresponding number of cards and finds the total amount of the coins shown. The player with the higher amount keeps his cards. The other player returns his set to the playing surface.
4. If players' coins total the same amount, all cards are returned.
5. Play continues until players cannot take the number of cards indicated by the die. The player with more cards at the end of the game wins.

©The Education Center, Inc.

# Coin Cards

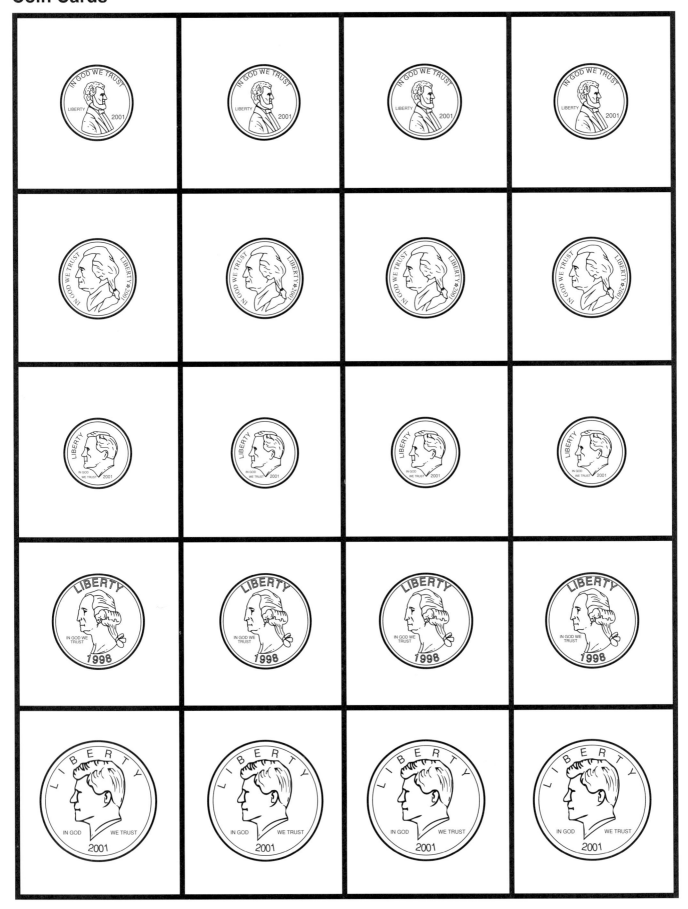

# Penny Pinchers

**Skill:** making change

**Number of players:** 2

**Materials for each pair:**
- copy of the cards on page 64 (cut out)
- 50 penny manipulatives

**Teacher preparation:**

Before playing the game, have each student look at a game card. Point out that the tag shows the price of the snack. The coins show the amount paid.

**Object of the game:**

to collect more pennies by making change

## Playing the game:

1. Stack the game cards facedown. Place the pennies next to the stack.
2. Player 1 draws a card and studies it.
3. Player 1 uses the pennies to count up from the price to the amount paid and keeps those pennies.
4. Player 2 takes a turn in the described manner.
5. Play continues until all the cards have been drawn. The player to collect more pennies wins.

## Variation:

To review making change from larger amounts, reprogram each card with a lower price. Provide each pair with penny, nickel, and dime manipulatives. The player with less coins at the end of the game wins.

**Game Cards**

©The Education Center, Inc. • *Games Galore* • *Math* • TEC2513

# Change Is Good

**Skill:** making change

**Number of players:** 2

**Materials for each pair:**

- copy of the gameboard and game cards on page 66 (cut out)
- set of coin manipulatives or copy of the coin cards on page 62 (cut out)
- 2 game markers

**Object of the game:**

to be the first player to get to the mall exit by counting change from purchases

## Playing the game:

1. Place the game cards facedown on the gameboard. Then place the game markers at "Toys 4 Kids."
2. In turn, each player draws a card. Using the coins to help him, he counts up from the price shown on the space to the amount shown on his card. He calculates his change, discards the card, then moves forward zero, one, or two spaces as indicated by the rules on the gameboard.
3. Play continues in this manner. Players shuffle the cards and reuse them as needed.
4. The first person to go around the gameboard and reach "Mall Exit" wins.

## Variation:

For practice comparing money amounts, players draw a card and compare the amount paid with the price. If the amount paid is greater than the price, the player advances one space. If the amount paid is equal to or less than the price, he remains at the space. The first player to reach "Mall Exit" wins.

# Gameboard

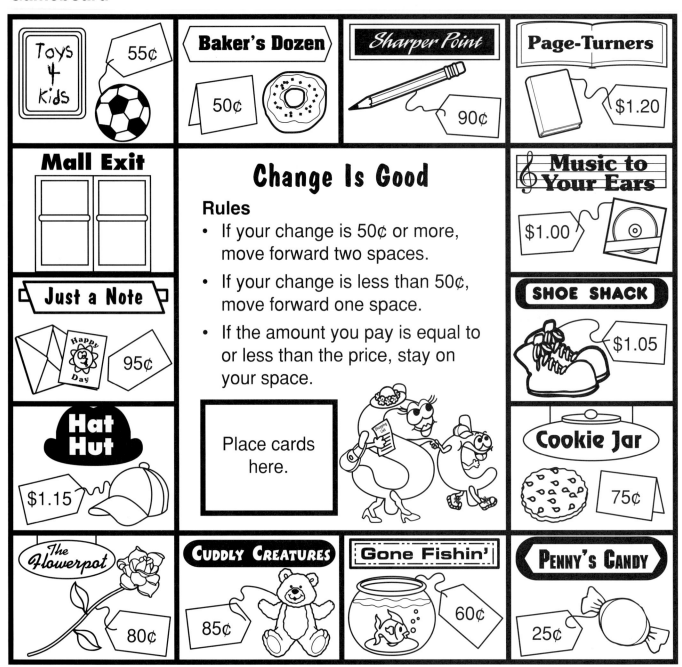

**Change Is Good**

**Rules**
- If your change is 50¢ or more, move forward two spaces.
- If your change is less than 50¢, move forward one space.
- If the amount you pay is equal to or less than the price, stay on your space.

Place cards here.

Toys 4 Kids — 55¢

Baker's Dozen — 50¢

Sharper Point — 90¢

Page-Turners — $1.20

Mall Exit

Music to Your Ears — $1.00

Just a Note — 95¢

Shoe Shack — $1.05

Hat Hut — $1.15

Cookie Jar — 75¢

The Flowerpot — 80¢

Cuddly Creatures — 85¢

Gone Fishin' — 60¢

Penny's Candy — 25¢

## Game Cards

| | | | | |
|---|---|---|---|---|
| Pay $1.00. | Pay $1.00. | Pay $1.00. | Pay $1.00. | Pay $1.00. |
| Pay $1.25. | Pay $1.25. | Pay $1.50. | Pay $1.75. | Pay $1.75. |

# Googly-Eyed Graphing

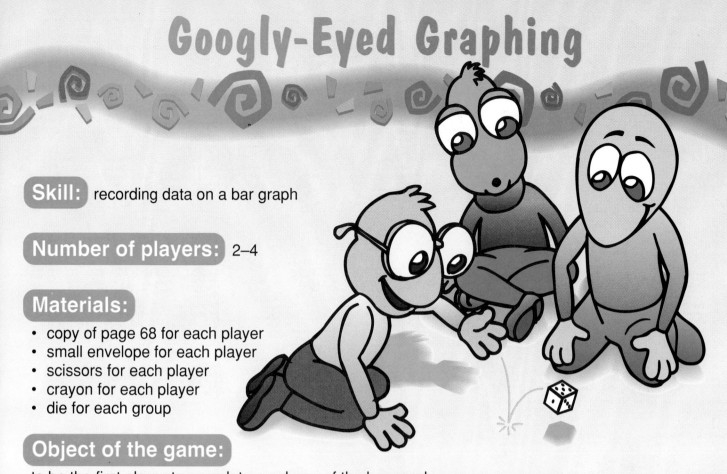

**Skill:** recording data on a bar graph

**Number of players:** 2–4

**Materials:**
- copy of page 68 for each player
- small envelope for each player
- scissors for each player
- crayon for each player
- die for each group

**Object of the game:**

to be the first player to complete a column of the bar graph

## Playing the game:
1. Each player cuts out his game cards and places them in his envelope.
2. Player 1 rolls the die, randomly takes the corresponding number of cards from his envelope, and colors in his graph to show which cards were picked.
3. Player 1 returns his cards to the envelope. Then the next player takes a turn in the same manner.
4. Alternate play continues until one player wins the game by completely filling one column of the graph.

©The Education Center, Inc.

## Variation:

For more challenging graphing practice, reprogram the graph on page 68 so that the value of each space is numbered by twos instead of ones and then duplicate the page for students.

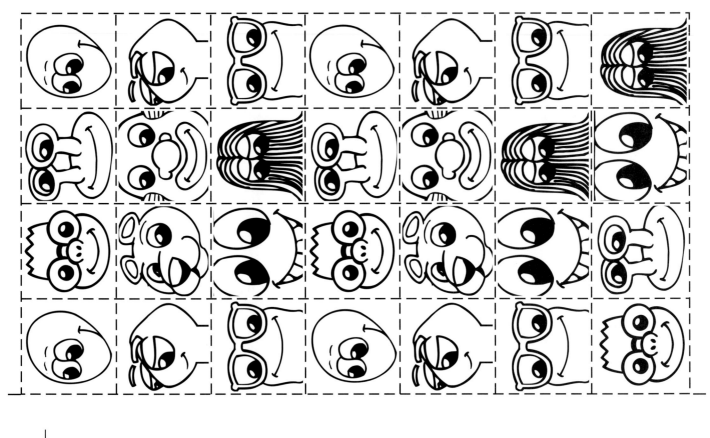

Player _____

## Googly-Eyed Graphing

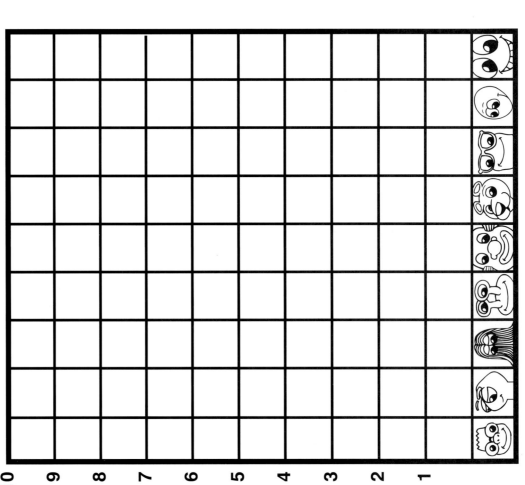

10
9
8
7
6
5
4
3
2
1

# Shark Attack!

**Skill:** using coordinates to plot points on a grid

**Number of players:** 2

**Materials for each pair:**
- copy of page 70
- 2 different-colored dice
- several small game pieces (such as buttons or beans)

**Object of the game:**
to win more rounds out of five by not landing
on coordinate points marked by sharks

**Playing the game:**
1. Players sit at opposite ends of the gameboard. Then each labels her gameboard to identify the direction each die represents (for example, → = white and ↑ = blue).
2. In turn, a player rolls the dice, uses the key to find the coordinates, and places a game marker on her grid at the matching point.
3. If the matching point is a dot, the player is safe. If the matching point is a shark, the round is over and the other player earns a point for the round.
4. At the end of each round, the winning player tallies her point in her score box.
5. The first player to earn three points wins the game.

**Variation:**

For more challenging practice with coordinates, distribute to each player his half of the gameboard. Have players hide their gameboards from view. To play, Player 1 guesses a location. If the location hits a shark on Player 2's gameboard, Player 1 tallies a point in his score box. Alternate play continues in this manner until one player earns four points by hitting all of his opponent's sharks. To avoid duplication of guesses, encourage players to mark the coordinate points they call on their gameboards.

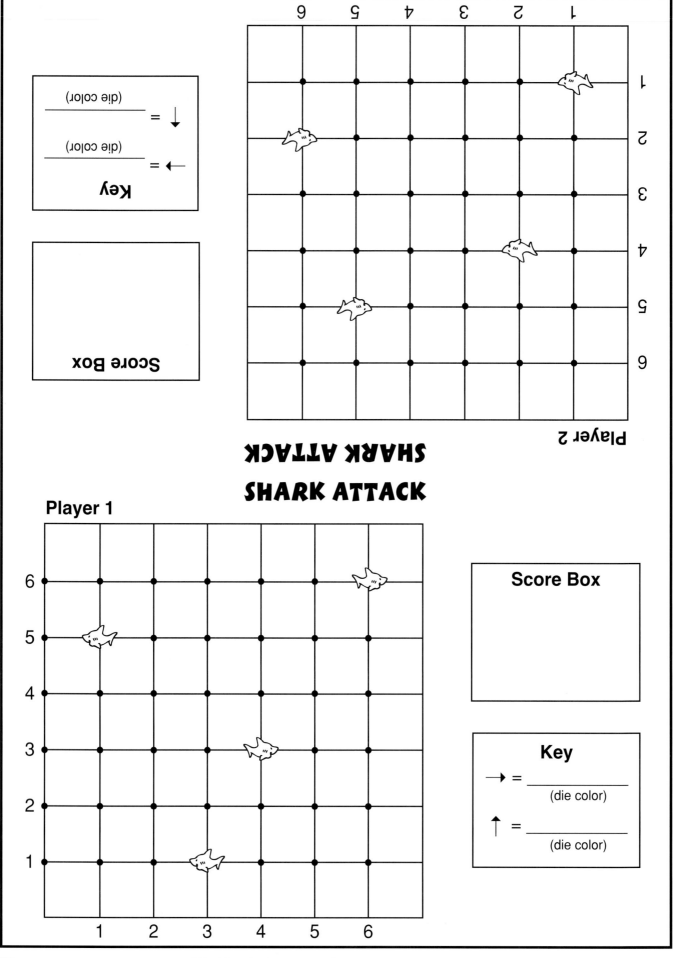

SHARK ATTACK

**Player 1**

Score Box

Key

→ = _____
(die color)

↑ = _____
(die color)

©The Education Center, Inc. • *Games Galore • Math* • TEC2513

# Probability Pups

**Skill:** predicting outcomes

**Number of players:** 2

**Materials:**
- copy of gameboard and pup patterns on page 72 (cut out) for each player
- pair of number cubes for each pair

**Object of the game:**

to be the first player to remove all the pups from the houses on his gameboard by predicting sums that will most likely be rolled

## Playing the game:
1. Each player thinks of possible sums that can be rolled by the number cubes and strategically places his pups in the houses of his choice. (Players may place several pups in some houses.)
2. In turn, each player rolls the cubes, adds the numbers shown, and removes one pup from the house that matches the sum.
3. If the player does not have a pup in the corresponding house, his turn is over.
4. The first player to remove all the pups from the houses wins.

## Variation:

Use self-adhesive dots to reprogram one number cube with numbers 7–12. The game is played as described, except each player removes a pup from the house that matches the difference shown on the cubes.

**Gameboard**

# Probability Pups

©The Education Center, Inc.

**Pup Patterns**

©The Education Center, Inc. • *Games Galore* • *Math* • TEC2513

# Spin to Win!

**Skill:** finding probability using spinners

**Number of players:** 2

**Materials for each pair:**
- copy of page 74
- small paper clip
- pencil

**Object of the game:**

to be the first player to complete all ten tasks in order by choosing the spinner with the better probability

**Playing the game:**

1. Player 1 reads the directions for the first task, chooses a spinner that is more likely to stop on the appropriate number, and uses the pencil and paper clip to spin the spinner.
2. If the spinner stops on the appropriate number, Player 1 checks the appropriate column to show that the task has been completed. If it does not stop on the appropriate number, her turn is over and the player must try again on her next spin.
3. Player 2 takes a turn in the described manner.
4. Players alternate turns, advancing to the next task as each is completed.
5. The first player to complete all ten tasks wins the game.

©The Education Center, Inc.

Player 1 _____     Player 2 _____

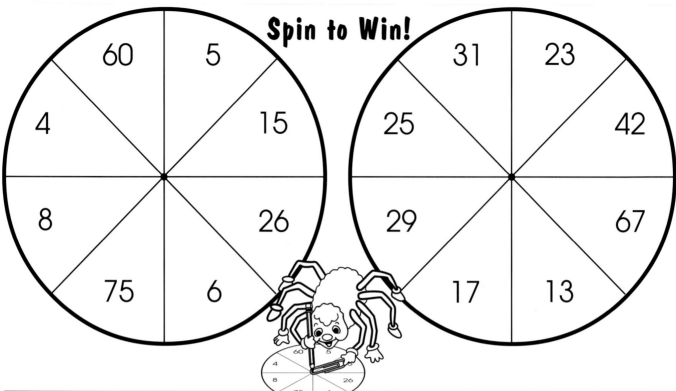

Spin to Win!

| Task Directions | Completed Tasks | |
| --- | --- | --- |
| | Player 1 | Player 2 |
| 1.  Spin an odd number. | | |
| 2.  Spin a number less than 12. | | |
| 3.  Spin a one-digit number. | | |
| 4.  Spin a number that has a 6. | | |
| 5.  Spin a number with 2 in the tens place. | | |
| 6.  Spin an even number. | | |
| 7.  Spin a number with 5 in the ones place. | | |
| 8.  Spin a number greater than 50. | | |
| 9.  Spin a number between 12 and 19. | | |
| 10.  Spin a number between 30 and 40. | | |

# Insect Inspector

**Skill:** identifying patterns

**Number of players:** 2

**Materials for each pair:**
- construction paper copy of page 76
- copy of the answer key on page 95 (optional)
- 4" x 4" piece of tagboard
- small metal brad
- paper clip
- scissors
- glue

**Teacher preparation:**
1. Instruct one student in each pair to assemble the spinner. Have him cut out the spinner pattern and glue it to the tagboard. Then direct him to insert the brad through the paper clip and then through the spinner.
2. Have the other student in each pair cut apart the insect strips and place them facedown on the playing surface.
3. If desired, provide each pair with a copy of the answer key to check disputed answers.

**Object of the game:**

to earn more insect strips by correctly identifying patterns

**Playing the game:**
1. Player 1 turns five strips faceup.
2. Player 1 spins the spinner and keeps each strip that features the pattern shown.
3. If Player 1 misses a strip, Player 2 may challenge the turn and pick up any matching strips left behind. The remaining strips are then turned facedown.
4. Player 2 takes a turn in the same manner.
5. Alternate play continues until there are less than five strips. The player who has collected more strips by this point wins the game.

**Insect Strips**

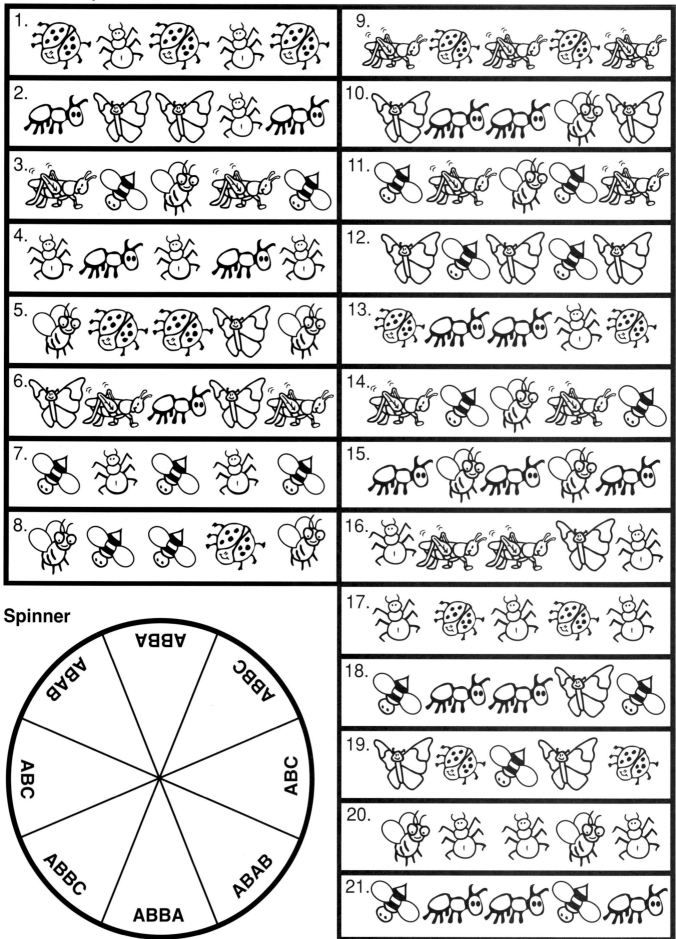

**Spinner**

# Unlocking Patterns

**Skill:** identifying pattern rules

**Number of players:** whole class divided into pairs

**Materials:**
- laminated key for each pair (pattern on page 78)
- transparency of the numeric and geometric patterns on page 78
- copy of the answer key on page 95
- erasable marker for each pair
- paper towel for each pair
- access to an overhead projector
- sheet of paper

**Object of the game:**

to accumulate the most points by correctly identifying pattern rules

**Playing the game:**
1. Display the transparency containing the numeric and geometric patterns. Cover the transparency so that only the first pattern is shown.
2. Ask students, "Who can unlock this pattern?"
3. Within a predetermined amount of time, partners confer, determine the pattern rule, and write the rule on their key with the erasable marker.
4. When time is up, reveal the pattern rule shown on the answer key.
5. If a pair is correct, the partners tally one point on their key.
6. All players wipe the pattern rules from their keys before the next pattern is shown.
7. Continue play in the same manner until all the patterns have been used. The pair with the highest amount of points wins. If more than one team receives the highest number of points, the game is a tie.

**Variations:**

For more pattern practice, have students write the next symbol or number in the pattern. Or have students create lists of new patterns and rules to use for additional rounds of play.

**Key Pattern**

**Numeric and Geometric Patterns**

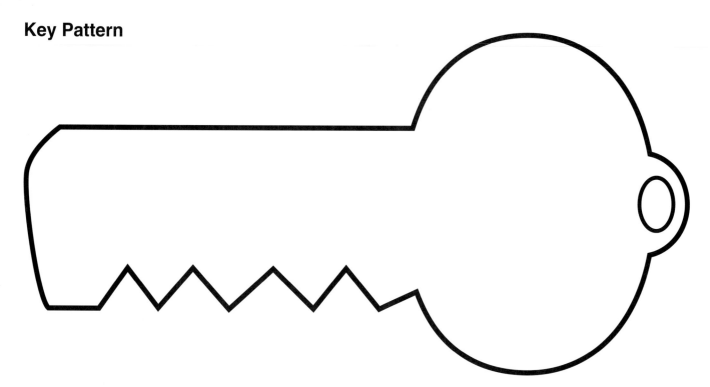

# Number Detective

**Skill:** finding missing addends

**Number of players:** 3

**Materials for each group:**
- 2 construction paper copies of the number cards on page 80 (cut out)
- calculator (optional)

**Object of the game:**

to collect more cards by correctly identifying the missing addend

**Playing the game:**
1. Each group selects one person to be the caller.
2. The caller shuffles the cards and deals them to the two players.
3. Each player stacks his cards facedown.
4. At the caller's signal, each player draws a card and, without looking at it, places it on his forehead so that the other player can see the number.
5. The caller announces the sum of the two numbers on the cards. (He may use a calculator to verify the sum if desired.)
6. Using the number shown, each player determines the value of his number. The first player to identify his number keeps both cards.
7. Play continues until all cards have been drawn. The player who collects more cards wins and becomes the new caller.

©The Education Center, Inc.

**Variation:**

For multiplication practice, have the caller announce the product of the two numbers drawn. Each player then guesses the missing factor.

**Number Cards**

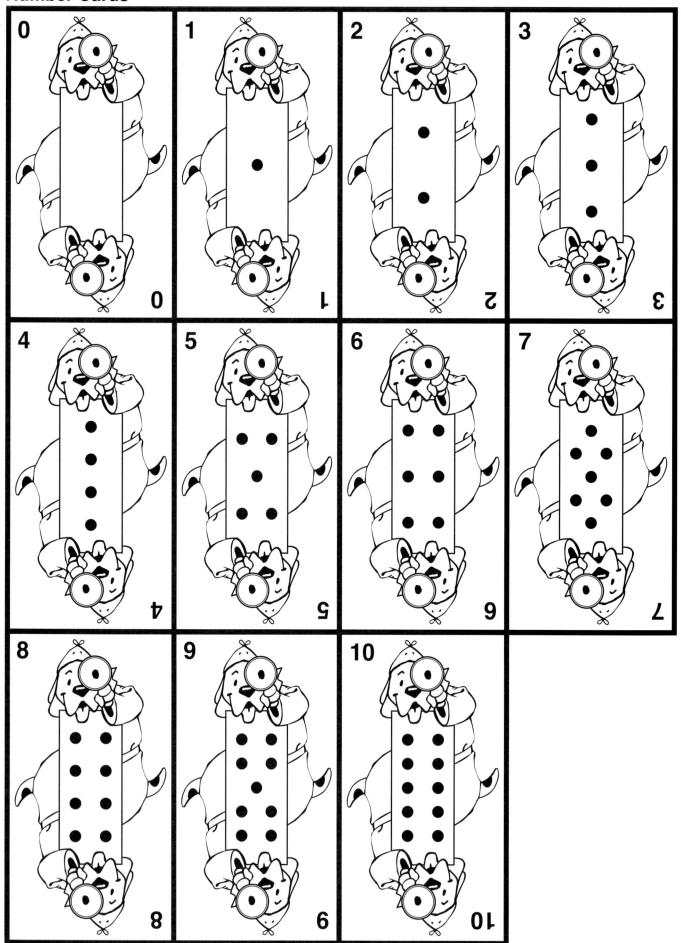

# Creature Feature

**Skill:** drawing simple shapes

**Number of players:** 2–4

**Materials:**
- pair of prepared creature cubes for each group
- drawing paper for each player
- pencil for each player

**Teacher preparation:**
1. Make a copy of the cube patterns on page 82 for each group of players.
2. Assemble the cubes for students as directed.
3. Because the drawing of body parts will be in random order, notify students that they may erase and redraw body parts as needed. Also encourage creative placement of parts as students draw their creatures.

**Object of the game:**

to be the first student to complete a drawing of a creature that includes a body, a head, arms and hands, legs and feet, eyes and a nose, and a mouth

---

**Playing the game:**
1. In turn, roll the creature cubes.
2. Draw the matching body part(s) for your creature in the shape shown.
3. If a player rolls a body part that has already been drawn, his turn is over.
4. Alternate play continues until one player wins the game by drawing a creature complete with a body, a head, arms and hands, legs and feet, eyes and a nose, and a mouth.

---

**Variation:**

For more challenging practice, white-out the shapes on the shape creature cube so that students will have to read the word name for each shape. Or reprogram the cube so that it includes words and/or pictures for more complex shapes, such as a trapezoid, pentagon, or hexagon.

**Directions:**

1. Carefully cut out the cube patterns along the outside edges.
2. Fold the patterns along each uncut line to form cubes.
3. Glue each tab inside each cube.

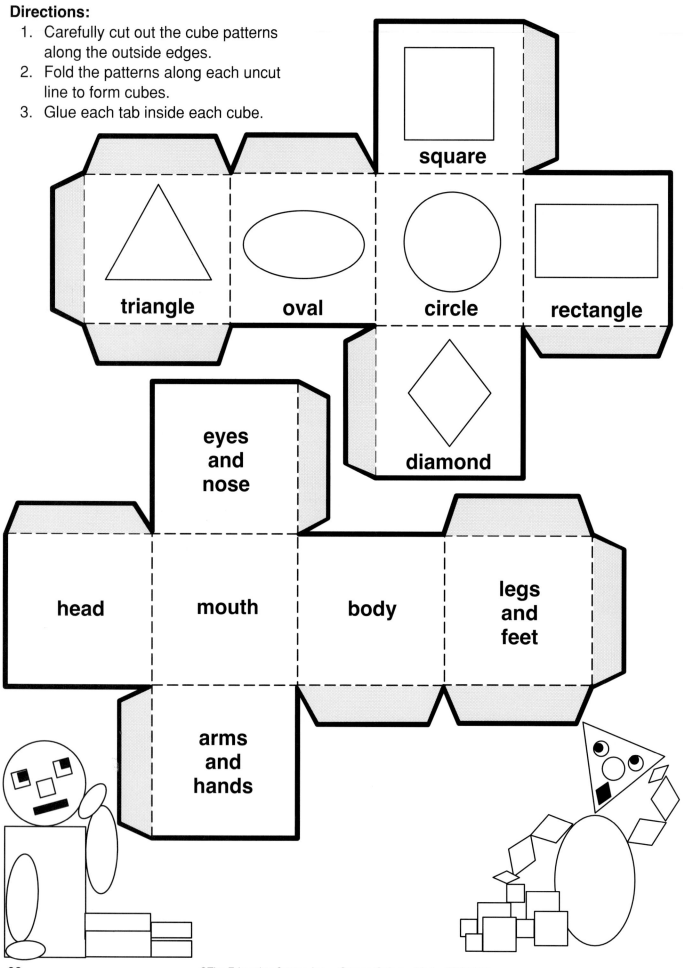

square

triangle

oval

circle

rectangle

diamond

eyes and nose

head

mouth

body

legs and feet

arms and hands

# Shape Up!

**Skills:** identifying plane figures

**Number of players:** 2

**Materials for each pair:**
- copy of page 84
- game marker
- 2 crayons
- die

**Object of the game:**

to be the first player to color all of the shapes in his section of the gameboard

## Playing the game:
1. To begin, place the game marker on any gameboard space.
2. In turn, each player rolls the die and moves clockwise the corresponding number of spaces.
3. The player reads the word he lands on, finds the matching shape in his section of the gameboard, and colors it.
4. Each player may color only one shape per turn.
5. Alternate play continues until one player wins by coloring all of the shapes in his section of the gameboard.

©The Education Center, Inc.

## Variation:

For more practice with plane figures, white-out the word *circle* on the gameboard and write the name of a plane figure not shown, such as *trapezoid*. Then white-out the circle in each player's section and draw the corresponding shape. Make copies of the gameboard for students to play the game in the same manner.

Player 1 _____  Player 2 _____

# Shape Up!

| | |
|---|---|
| square | rectangle |

pentagon

triangle

circle

triangle

hexagon

| | |
|---|---|
| rectangle | pentagon |

hexagon

## Player 1

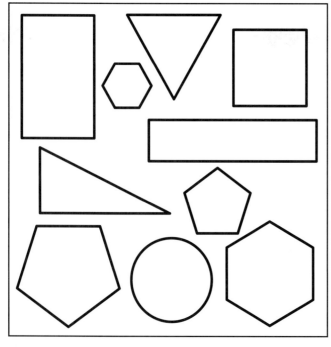

## Player 2

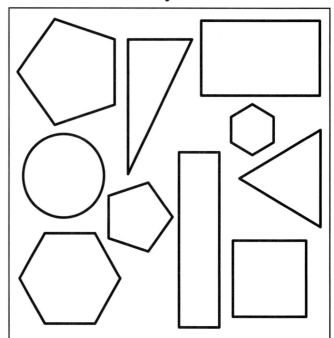

# Space Race

**Skill:** identifying solid figures

**Number of players:** 2

**Materials for each pair:**
- laminated copy of the gameboard on page 86
- 2 game markers
- paper clip
- pencil

**Object of the game:**
to reach the end of the gameboard by correctly identifying solid figures

**Playing the game:**
1. Players place their game markers on Start.
2. In turn, each player uses the pencil and paper clip to spin the spinner and moves forward to the closest corresponding figure on the gameboard.
3. If the figure is not ahead of the player's marker, her turn is over.
4. The first player to reach the last solid figure wins.

©The Education Center, Inc.

**Variation:**

To increase the difficulty level, reprogram the spinner with the numbers 0, 1, 2, 4, and 6. In turn, each player spins the spinner. She moves to the closest figure on the gameboard that has the corresponding number of faces.

# Space Race

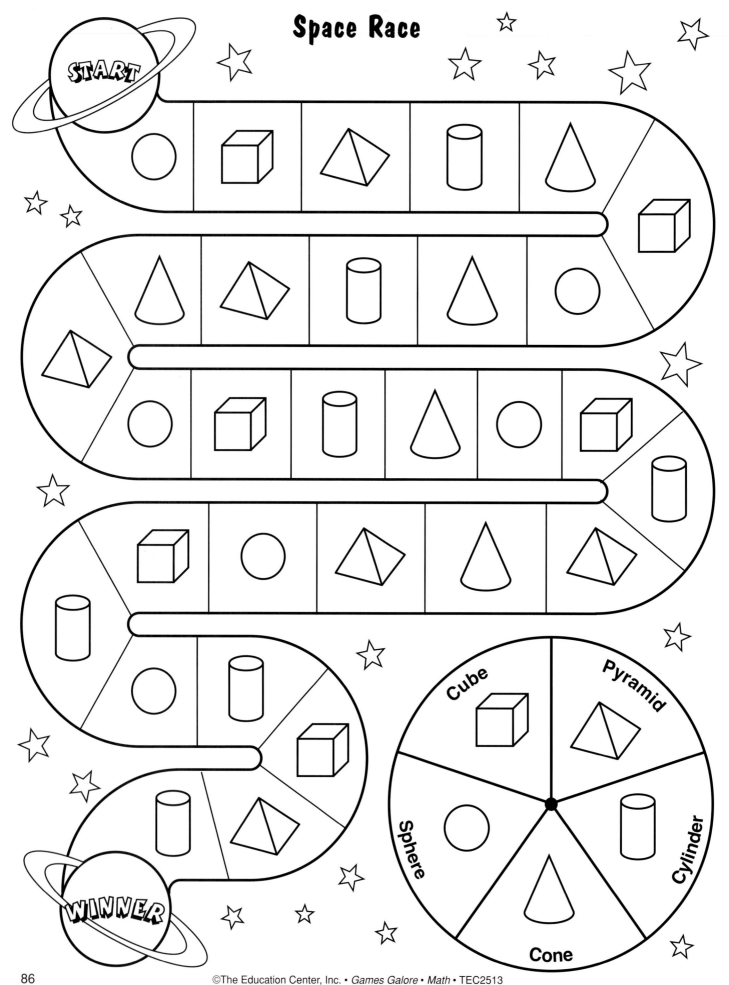

# Geometric Gymnasts

**Skill:** identifying slides, flips, and turns

**Number of players:** 2

**Materials for each pair:**
- copy of page 88
- 2 game markers
- 2 prepared color tiles

**Teacher Preparation:**
1. Provide each pair with a copy of page 88 and have them cut out the squares at the bottom.
2. Direct the pair to tape the front and back of each bear to opposite sides of a tile as shown.
3. Then have students cut out their gameboard.

**Object of the game:**
to reach the end of the gameboard by correctly identifying slides, flips, and turns.

**Playing the game:**
1. Game markers are placed on Start.
2. Player 1 tosses the tiles and randomly pushes them together so that they are side by side.
3. Then Player 1 compares the bears and identifies the movement as a slide, flip, or turn. He moves his marker forward to the first corresponding space on the gameboard.
4. If no movement is shown, if more than one movement is shown (for example, a flip and a turn), or if the type of movement is not ahead of the player's marker, the player remains on his space.
5. Alternate play continues in this manner. The first player to toss a "turn" and reach the last space on the gameboard wins.

**Gameboard**

# Geometric Gymnasts

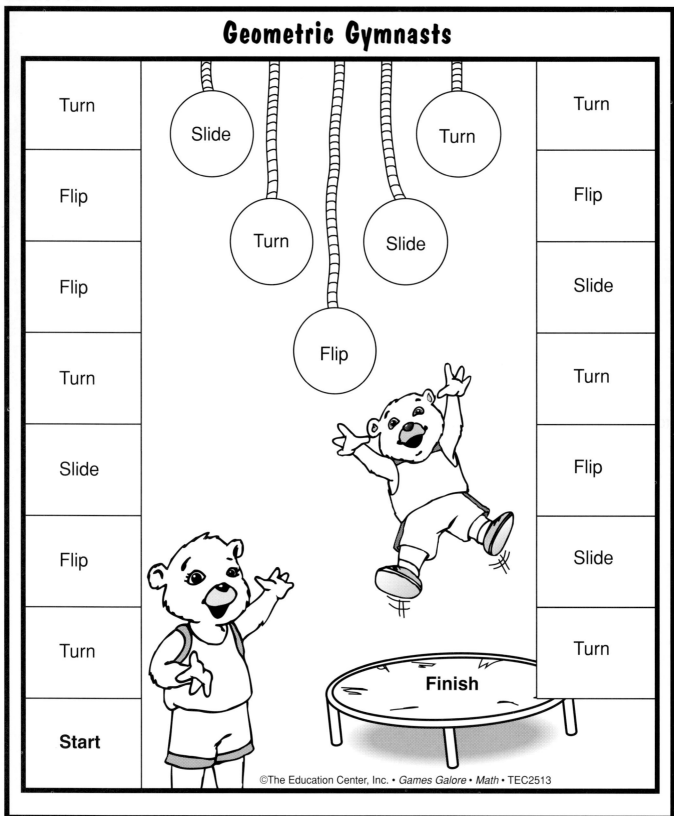

| | |
|---|---|
| Turn | Turn |
| Flip | Flip |
| Flip | Slide |
| Turn | Turn |
| Slide | Flip |
| Flip | Slide |
| Turn | Turn |
| **Start** | **Finish** |

Slide

Turn

Slide

Turn

Flip

©The Education Center, Inc. • *Games Galore* • *Math* • TEC2513

**Bear Patterns**

# Pigs in a Pen

**Skill:** logical reasoning

**Number of players:** 2

**Materials for each pair:**
- copy of the gameboard and pig game cards on page 90 (cut out)
- scratch paper
- pencil

**Object of the game:**

to win more rounds by placing the last pig in the pen

**Playing the game:**
1. For each round, place the pig cards in three rows of seven above the gameboard.
2. In turn, each player places one or two pigs in the pen.
3. Alternate play continues until one player places the last pig in the pen and wins a point.
4. The player who has more points at the end of five rounds wins the game.

©The Education Center, Inc.

**Variation:**

For more strategic play, have players place the pigs in the pen. Then players may pull one, two, or three pigs from the pen. After each pig has been pulled, the player with an odd number of pigs wins the round.

**Gameboard**

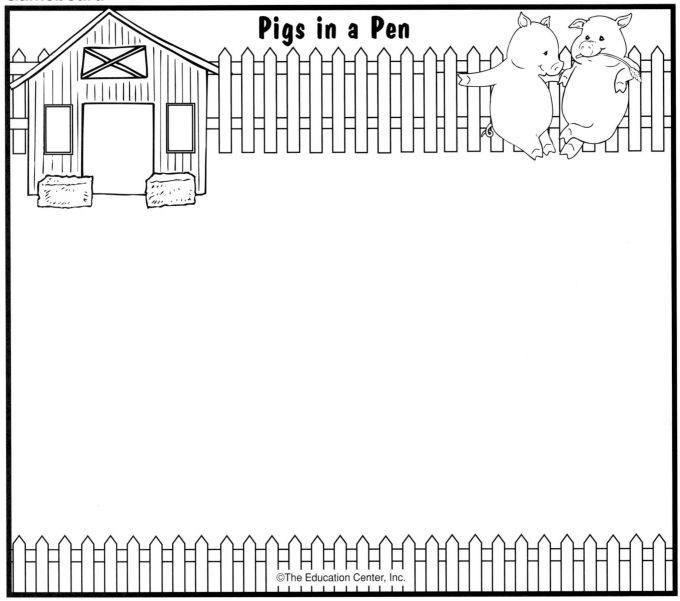

**Pig Cards**

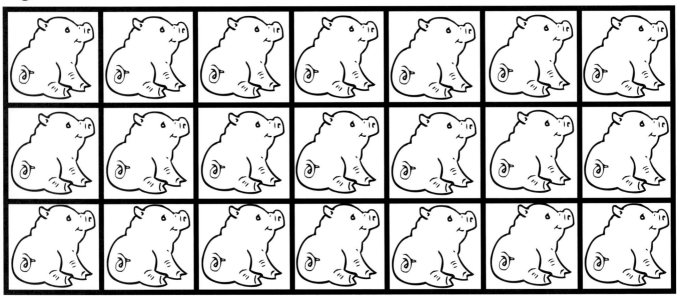

# Flipping Flapjacks

**Skill:** using logical reasoning

**Number of players:** 2

**Materials for each pair:**
- copy of page 92
- 12 two-color counters
- scratch paper
- pencil

**Object of the game:**
to win more rounds by completing vertical, horizontal, or diagonal rows of three counters displaying the same color

**Playing the game:**
1. Player 1 covers a flapjack on the griddle with a counter. Player 1 may place the counter to display either of the colors.
2. Player 2 takes a turn in the same manner.
3. As alternate play continues, each player may display either color on the counter he lays down.
4. The first player to complete a row of three in either color wins a point for the round and records his point on scratch paper.
5. The player who wins more rounds out of five wins the game.

©The Education Center, Inc.

# Flipping Flapjacks!

# Counting "Ant-ics"

**Skills:** using logical reasoning, strategy

**Number of players:** 2

**Materials for each pair:**
- copy of page 94
- 36 two-color counters

**Object of the game:**
to collect more counters on the home anthill

**Playing the game:**
1. Each player sits in front of his home anthill.
2. Each player stacks three counters in each of his circles.
3. In turn, each player takes the counters from any one of his circles. Moving clockwise, he stacks one counter on each gameboard space (circle or home anthill) until he runs out.
4. If Player 1's last counter lands on his home anthill, he takes another turn. If his last counter lands on an empty circle (even if it is Player 2's circle), he may take the counters (if any) from the circle directly across the gameboard and put them on his home anthill.
5. The game is over when a player runs out of counters in his circles. The player with more counters on his home anthill wins.

©The Education Center, Inc.

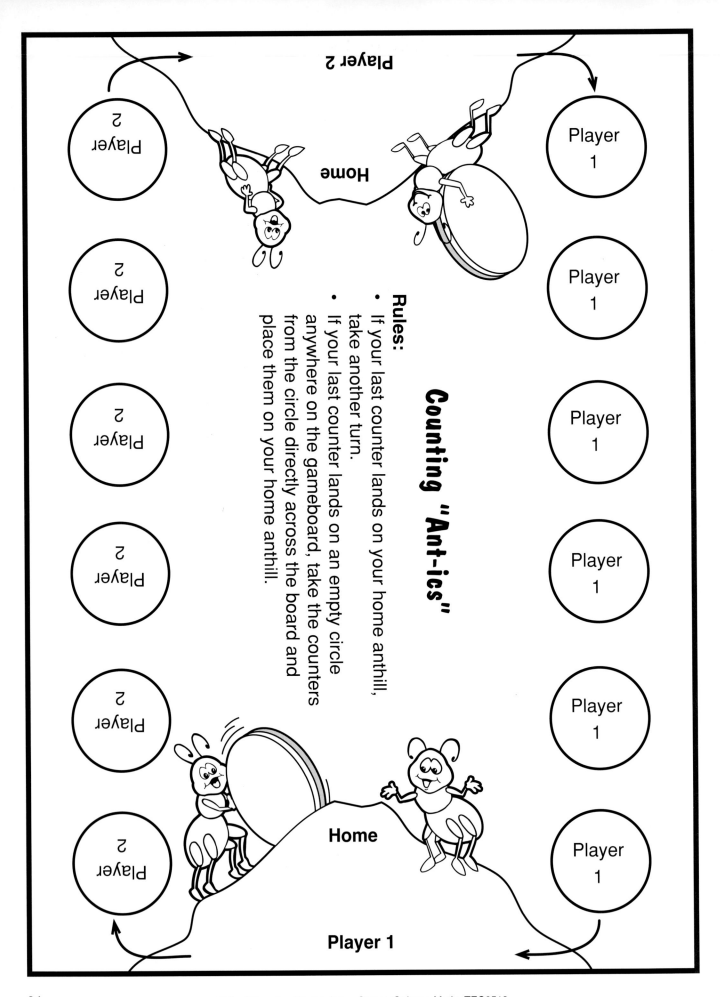

# Counting "Ant-ics"

**Rules:**
- If your last counter lands on your home anthill, take another turn.
- If your last counter lands on an empty circle anywhere on the gameboard, take the counters from the circle directly across the board and place them on your home anthill.

Player 2

Player 2

Player 2

Player 2

Player 2

Player 2

**Home**

Player 1

Player 1

Player 1

Player 1

Player 1

Player 1

**Home**

**Player 1**

# Answer Keys

## Page 50

1. ounces
2. ounces
3. pounds
4. pounds
5. pounds
6. pounds
7. pounds
8. ounces
9. pounds
10. ounces
11. ounces
12. ounces
13. ounces
14. pounds
15. pounds
16. ounces
17. pounds
18. pounds

## Page 76

1. ABAB
2. ABBC
3. ABC
4. ABAB
5. ABBC
6. ABC
7. ABAB
8. ABBC
9. ABAB
10. ABBC
11. ABC
12. ABAB
13. ABBC
14. ABC
15. ABAB
16. ABBC
17. ABAB
18. ABBC
19. ABC
20. ABBA
21. ABBA

## Page 78

One possible rule for each pattern is listed below.

A. count backward by fives
B. square, then circle, increasing by one each time
C. increase by one circle each time
D. add two each time
E. add two, then add three
F. number of circles added increases by one row each time to form a triangle
G. turn the point of the pentagon clockwise
H. add two, then subtract one
I. add two squares each time, one vertically and one horizontally
J. add zero, then subtract four

**Project Manager:** Njeri Jones Legrand
**Staff Editors:** Denine T. Carter, Diane F. McGraw
**Contributing Writers:** Amy Barsanti, Lisa Buchholz, Vicki Dabrowka, Kish Harris, Lucia Kemp Henry, Cynthia Holcomb, Linda Masternak Justice, Shelly Lanier, Kimberly Minafo, Valerie Wood Smith
**Copy Editors:** Sylvan Allen, Gina Farago, Karen Brewer Grossman, Karen L. Huffman, Amy Kirtley-Hill, Debbie Shoffner
**Cover Artists:** Nick Greenwood, Clevell Harris
**Art Coordinator:** Barry Slate
**Artists:** Pam Crane, Theresa Lewis Goode, Nick Greenwood, Clevell Harris, Sheila Krill, Clint Moore, Greg D. Rieves, Rebecca Saunders, Barry Slate, Donna K. Teal
**Typesetters:** Lynette Dickerson, Mark Rainey

**President, The Mailbox Book Company™:** Joseph C. Bucci
**Director of Book Planning and Development:** Chris Poindexter
**Book Development Managers:** Stephen Levy, Elizabeth H. Lindsay, Thad McLaurin, Susan Walker
**Curriculum Director:** Karen P. Shelton
**Traffic Manager:** Lisa K. Pitts
**Librarian:** Dorothy C. McKinney
**Editorial and Freelance Management:** Karen A. Brudnak
**Editorial Training:** Irving P. Crump
**Editorial Assistants:** Terrie Head, Hope Rodgers, Jan E. Witcher